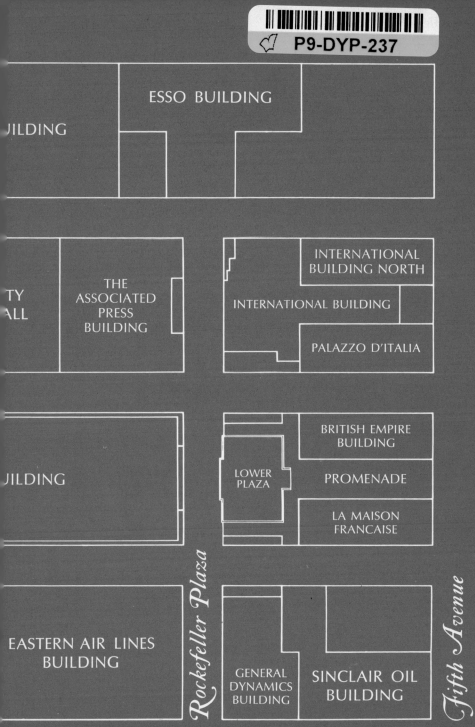

THE CITY WITHIN A CITY

Other Books by David Loth

THE CITY WITHIN A CITY:

The Romance of Rockefeller Center

David Loth

William Morrow & Company, *New York, 1966*

Published simultaneously in Canada
by George J. McLeod Limited, Toronto.

Printed in the United States of America.

Library of Congress Catalog Card Number 66-17182

Contents

Acknowledgments

The documents from which much of the information for this book was derived are from the Columbiana Collection at Columbia University and the files of Rockefeller Center. I am grateful to both institutions for making them available. In addition, the staff of the Society Library, as always, has been extremely helpful in providing data about New York.

But more important than the written record, in many ways, have been my conversations with some of the men and women who helped to build and operate Rockefeller Center. First of all, Caroline Hood, a Center vice-president, has answered questions, located papers, and arranged interviews with patience and good humor. Nelson A. Rockefeller, Winthrop Rockefeller, Wallace K. Harrison, G. S. Eyssell, Victor Borella, Russell V. Downing, and others of the staff have taken time out of their busy lives to talk of the early—and later—days and to answer questions. Finally, I am indebted to Norris Darrell of Sullivan & Cromwell for light on the lease once held by the firm's late senior partner.

DAVID LOTH

A Note on the Illustrations

The photograph of John D. Rockefeller, Jr. at his desk is reproduced with the permission of *Life* magazine. Wallace K. Harrison supplied from his own files the copy of his first sketch of the Metropolitan Opera project. All the other illustrations have been furnished by Rockefeller Center, Inc.

1

Mr. Rockefeller's Dilemma

December, 1929, was an awkward time whether a man had money or not—few did. The most disastrous stock market crash in-history was six weeks old, and the whole country felt that the rug had been pulled from under it. In New York, center of the financial and business world, this feeling was especially acute because here more than anywhere else people had believed that the secret of perpetual prosperity was theirs. Numb, dazed, and hysterical are words commonly used by historians of the Great Depression to describe the reaction of business and financial leaders to the sudden collapse. On every side these gentlemen were issuing hollow statements of reassurance while unostentatiously canceling plans for spending any money on expansion or improvement.

In December, 1929, the value of stocks listed on the New

York Exchange was only 60 percent of prices quoted in late September. The economy of the United States was grinding closer to a halt than ever before. It would be hard to imagine a worse time to be holding the bag for a loftily cultural, magnificently extravagant, utterly doomed building project.

On December 5, John D. Rockefeller, Jr., found himself in exactly this position! His name was signed at the bottom of a lease by which he stood committed to pay Columbia University at least $3.3 million a year for twenty-four years on thirteen acres of run-down, midtown real estate which at the moment brought in $300,000. A bite of this size was not to be contemplated without pain, even by a Rockefeller.

True, many similar promises to pay were unredeemable in the aftermath of the stock market crash. But not this one. Only a couple of weeks earlier this point had been underlined when the elder John D. Rockefeller, in his first public statement in almost a generation, had tried to inspire a little confidence in the economy.

"Believing that fundamental conditions of the country are sound," he declared from the fastness of Pocantico Hills, the 3,500-acre family estate above the Hudson, "my son and I have for some days been purchasing sound common stocks."

"Sure," Eddie Cantor asked wryly, "who else had any money left?"

The lessee of Columbia's midtown property was worrying less about the money, to be sure, than about the project that that money represented. This was nothing less than an ambitious cultural and commercial center to be built around a new home for the Metropolitan Opera. Now the Opera Company, the key to the enterprise, had bowed out, one of the cogent reasons being that it was not among those who had any money left.

So in a dark, paneled office at 26 Broadway, sitting before an old-fashioned, roll-top desk which had been his father's, the heir to America's greatest fortune, and the Met's most recent problem, faced the dilemma of what to do with that twenty-four-year lease. At this time fifty-six years old, John D. Rockefeller, Jr., was one of the least known of the city's leaders. Unassuming and modest to the point of shyness, he had taken more pains than almost anyone of his generation to avoid public attention. Medium in height and build, he was almost indistinguishable from the general run of financial district clerks—almost, but not quite. If you looked closely, you might be struck by something a little unusual in the cut of the man's jaw and of his clothes. An extra ration of bone gave the regular, pleasant features more character than expected. The excellent quality of his tailoring, almost dandified, offset the unobtrusiveness of style by ever so slight a margin.

It was almost a year to the day of December 2, 1928, when he had formed a new company, appropriately named the Metropolitan Square Corporation, to develop a suitable setting for the Opera, whose quarters on Thirty-ninth Street and Broadway were even then considered to be outmoded. When, in January, 1929, the Corporation leased the Columbia land, which was most of the three blocks bounded by Forty-eighth and Fifty-first streets and Fifth and Sixth avenues the era of perpetual prosperity seemed to ensure a resounding success. For months before that, and ever since, architects and engineers and construction specialists had been working and reworking designs for one of the most ambitious building projects the city had ever known.

Plans had been drawn for a veritable complex of entertainment facilities—theaters for music, drama, comedy, variety, and movies as well as opera—plus splendid shops, luxury hotels, new department stores, and imposing offices. These were to be developed in a landscaped setting of plazas and promenades served by private streets and the absolute latest in traffic control. A few disastrous autumn weeks had changed everything.

On that Thursday, December 5, the full extent of the economic disaster was by no means clear to most people. Thousands of men and women who had been speculating in the stock market were wiped out, of course. Perhaps a million had suffered losses in varying degrees. But surely the fundamental business structure of the country was sound enough, no? Only two days earlier, President Herbert Hoover had virtually said as much in his first annual message to Congress. He had spoken of "overoptimism" leading to rash speculation. He had said that speculation was punished by depriving the losers of some luxuries and temporarily throwing some innocent people out of work. Yet in general, he saw only a "hesitation" in the forward progress of productive industry and commerce.

Eminent industrialists who retained a faint image of authority were equally reassuring. Charles M. Schwab, a typical rags-to-riches hero, first president of the United States Steel Company, later Chairman of Bethlehem Steel, intoned: "Never before has American business been as firmly entrenched for prosperity as it is today."

All this should have made the difficulties of the Opera project seem a temporary annoyance at worst. But Rockefeller was in a position to know that neither the President nor many of the industrial leaders who spoke so soothingly really believed their own words. They felt obliged to utter falsehoods, or anyway well rehearsed, insincere platitudes to allay public panic. Their real sentiments had been expressed in more gloomy, realistic terms which became generally known years later.

The President, for example, had a meeting on November 21 with a group of leading executives from some of the biggest American corporations, several of them considered

"Rockefeller companies." He told them frankly that the situation was far more serious than a mere stock market collapse. While he made no attempt to predict how long the crisis would last nor how far it would go, he expected a protracted period of severe losses. He hoped that the business community would avoid the policy of previous depressions, which had been to "liquidate" labor. Hoover urged a more enlightened plan of maintaining wages and employment, even at a sacrifice of profits. Those who heard him, and those who were in the confidence of those who heard him, could hardly doubt that the country was in for massive business retrenchment.

Under the circumstances, Rockefeller must have known that the Opera Company's decision was no momentary setback. On the other hand, his father's statement in November about faith in the United States, which had scrupulously avoided any expression of confidence in immediate prospects for recovery, embodied the son's sincere belief. It was that, indeed, which made his dilemma difficult.

If he had shared the despairing view of those who saw the doom of the capitalist system, there would have been little point in trying to do anything at all with his lease on Columbia's land. If he had held to the rosy optimism of those who thought that only gamblers were going to suffer the penalties of the market, he might have waited for the Opera's backers to regain their courage and the old opera house its resale value. Two reasons for the Met's withdrawal had been the reluctance of the rich to commit themselves to large contributions, and the obvious impossibility of selling the old building for anything approaching the cost of a new one.

It is clear that his rejection of both the pessimistic and optimistic extremes of the day's opinions about the economic crisis dictated his decision on how to grapple with his dilemma. The first step on this Thursday was a public statement issued jointly with the Opera Company to announce the Met's withdrawal. It shared the front pages of Friday's newspapers with the organization in Washington of an economic council of four hundred business and industrial leaders, invited by Hoover to stabilize the country. Buried on the financial pages in the back without so much as a headline was information about a sharp little break in the stock market. It reflected the business reaction to the President's budget indicating a big surplus, to Secretary of the Treasury Mellon's proposal that the surplus reduce taxes rather than the national debt, and to the new reassurances of the economic council.

What turned out in the end to be the best economic news of the day was a paragraph tucked away at the bottom of the Opera story on an inside page of *The New York Times*. It simply noted that Rockefeller was going ahead with plans to develop the Columbia property. There was no indication in his statement of the form this development would take. However, the loss of the Opera was hardly a bolt from the blue. Rockefeller and his advisers had been thinking about possible alternatives for several weeks.

These alternatives presented only a choice of risks. The one man who could settle on which risk to assume was he who would have to pay for it, the quiet man in the paneled office at 26 Broadway. Clearly, he had made his choice before it was irrevocably imparted to the official records. For on December 6 it was so documented. That day the minutes of a board meeting of the Metropolitan Square Corporation noted that the management had instructed its distinguished body of architects "that from now on the Square should be based upon a commercial center as beautiful as possible consistent with the maximum income that could be developed."

2

Dr. Hosack's Garden

Rockefeller's mandate to his architects proposed a restoration in a sense, the recapturing in a new form of an earlier splendor. The acres of run-down brownstones which he was leasing had entered the view of history as one of the prized beauty spots of the Western World. That was in 1801 when a leading city physician and social lion decided to create the first botanical garden in New York.

Dr. David Hosack, "an eminently clubbable man," as Van Wyck Brooks called him, was a native son who had studied in London and Edinburgh as well as at Columbia, Princeton, and Pennsylvania. Soon after his return from abroad and before he was thirty, he made such a reputation during the yellow fever epidemic of 1797 that Dr. Samuel Bard, acknowledged head of New York's medical profession, took him into partnership. Dr. Hosack was also a professor of both botany and *materia medica* at Columbia College. A large, robust, hearty young gentleman whose Saturday evenings were the talk of the town, he was wildly extravagant. So when first Columbia and then the state refused to finance a botanical garden, he undertook to do it himself.

By this time there was not much vacant public land left on Manhattan below what is now Fifty-ninth Street. But almost three miles from the northern limits of the city, then at Chambers Street, the young doctor found a tract of twenty rocky, hilly, wooded acres which still belonged to New York. It fronted on Middle Road, the best carriage route leading north, and extended to within one hundred feet of the narrower Albany Road to the west. The tract consisted of lots Numbers 54, 55, 60, and 61 of the common lands, and the city fathers accepted $4,807.36 in cash plus a quit rent of sixteen bushels of good, merchantable wheat each year or the equivalent in cash. In 1810 Dr. Hosack paid $285.71 for a release from the quit rent, so the land cost just over $5,000.

It was a lonely spot. The thin soil and superabundant rocks had discouraged farmers. Chelsea to the southwest and Yorkville to the northeast were the nearest villages; Greenwich Village and Harlem were the only other two on Manhattan. But Dr. Hosack thought that trees, bushes, and herbs would thrive there, and he was right.

By the time the doctor accompanied his friends, Alexander Hamilton and Aaron Burr, to Weehawken in 1804, and treated Hamilton for the fatal wound he incurred there, his Elgin Botanical Garden, named for his father's birthplace in Scotland, was one of the wonders of New York. People used to drive out to see the two thousand different plants collected from all over the world. They could take a guided tour of the premises, entirely enclosed within a wall seven feet high by two and a half feet thick, made from stone collected in clearing and planting the property. Toward the

The Elgin Botanic Garden at its peak of popularity about 1808. The drawing is by an unknown illustrator.

northeast corner, between what are now Fiftieth and Fifty-first streets and not far in from Fifth Avenue, which Middle Road eventually was called, the doctor built two large hot-houses and a greenhouse. Radiating from these were the beds of flowers, herbs, and vegetables. Shrubs and a nursery encir-cled them, and the rest of the property except for a bit of pasture was planted with hundreds of varieties of trees, in-cluding the finest fruits known. It was, said one of the doctor's pupils and friends, all done "with princely munifi-cence" so that it had become "a resort for the admirers of nature's vegetable wonders and for the students of her mys-teries."

Dr. Hosack expended more than $100,000; it would cost a couple of million or more to achieve the same effect today. A visit to the garden ranked in popular favor with picnics to the Kissing Bridge on the Boston Post Road or fishing parties on the East River or snipe shooting in the marshes and meadows around Chelsea. Hamilton used to break the long ride between his Wall Street office and his country home, on what is now One Hundred Forty-fifth Street, at the hospitable Hosack house off Middle Road. The Duke of Saxe Weimar was entranced by the beauty of the garden, although he gave more space in the diary of his American tour to the Hosack evening parties in town.

The doctor reserved his own keenest enthusiasm for classes he taught in the garden. After 1807, when he and a few others founded the College of Physicians and Surgeons, his Columbia courses in botany and *materia medica* were augmented by lectures and demonstrations to the medical students. They in turn flocked to him. One of the first Americans to use a stethoscope, he was an early advocate of vaccination and a pioneer in limiting the bleeding of patients for any and all illnesses. He had become interested in botany through the great number of medicinal herbs which the science of his time was discovering. Therefore, he designed the Elgin Botanical Garden as a teaching aid as well as a tourist attraction. In fact, he expected to finance his beauty spot by selling medicinal plants as well as the produce from nursery and orchard.

He also expected the city or state or college, or maybe all three, to contribute a modest subsidy too. That support never materialized, and sales were far from meeting the lavish manner in which the doctor maintained his property. Within a year of the foundation of the College of Physicians and Surgeons, he was no longer able to afford the expense. Reluctantly, he petitioned the state to buy it, but at first there was little enthusiasm. Finally, in 1810, the legislature agreed to purchase the estate at a figure to be fixed by its own commissioners.

They appraised the garden, buildings and all, at $74,-

268.75. The act authorizing acquisition at that price also stipulated that no public funds were to be spent on maintenance. Yet doctors and students were to have free access at all times because the garden was "for the benefit of the medical schools of this state."

Under these restrictions, the state appointed the College of Physicians and Surgeons, which was not yet part of Columbia, to manage the estate in the interest of the medical profession. The college promptly leased land and buildings for five years to one of Dr. Hosack's gardeners, Richard Denison. He was to keep the garden in good condition and compensate himself through the sale of produce.

Although trustees complained that students and teachers had to travel too far to reach the garden, classes conducted there by Dr. Hosack and others on the College of Physicians and Surgeons faculty remained a feature of New York's medical instruction. The college's *Syllabus of Courses* for 1814 boasted in a passage describing *materia medica:* "For practical lessons on genera and species, the grand establishment of Elgin . . . is visited as often as necessary."

The "grand establishment" was losing its grandeur without the spendthrift guidance of Dr. Hosack. Guides no longer took admiring parties of nature lovers through the hothouses and grounds. Denison, understandably, was more interested in marketable fruits and plants than in beauty. Within two years of his sale, Dr. Hosack complained that fences and buildings badly needed repairs; valuable plants had disappeared. He had not abandoned his dream, and he drew up an elaborate program for the state, to be put into effect "as soon as measures may be taken for the permanent preservation of the Botanic Garden."

The legislature, however, had exhausted its interest in the project when it voted the purchase. Far from debating the public benefits to be derived from a state-supported botanical garden, the solons saw in this property the means of silencing an embarrassingly importunate suitor, Columbia College. This institution's trustees were men who could not be denied altogether, although they mustered less political muscle than the supporters of Columbia's newer rivals upstate. Even so early, the claims of New York City were subordinated to those of smaller communities.

The college had been rebuffed a number of times in its pleas for state aid, and now in 1814 it was petitioning for a share in the benefits to flow from "an act instituting a lottery for the promotion of literature and for other purposes." Lotteries were a favorite means of financing educational progress in those days. This one was earmarked primarily to assist Union College in Schenectady. Other institutions demanded some part of the proceeds too, and while none of them had as much influence as Union College, a few were favored. As finally passed, the act allotted $200,000 to Union College, $40,000 to Hamilton College, $30,000 to the College of Physicians and Surgeons, and $4,000 to the Ashbury Colored Church of New York. And Columbia? To the great disappointment of the trustees, not a dollar. But Section VI of the act provided:

That all the right, title and interest of the People of the State in and to all that certain piece or parcel of land situate in the 9th Ward of the City of New York known by the name of the Botanic Garden and lately conveyed to the People by David Hosack, be and the same is hereby granted to and vested in the Trustees of Columbia College; but this grant is made upon the express condition that the college establishment shall be removed to the said tract of land hereby granted, or to lands adjacent thereto, within twelve years from this time.

The legislature's only reference to Hosack's dream was Section VII, which stipulated:

The Trustees of the College, within 3 months shall transmit to the trustees of the other colleges of the State a list of the different kinds of plants, flowers and shrubs in the said garden, and within one year thereafter deliver at the said garden, if required, at least one healthy exotic flower, shrub or plant of each kind of which they shall have more than one at the time of application, together with the jar or vessel containing the same, to the trustees of each of the other colleges who shall apply therefor.

The *History of Columbia University* comments in a classical bit of understatement that this grant "was not considered by the trustees an attractive or helpful gift." These gentlemen, although considering a move from the Park Place land presented to Columbia at the time of its founding in 1754, felt themselves in need of hard money, not unproductive gardens. Nor did it seem reasonable to expect the college to build on a site so remote that many thought it too far from the city even for an occasional class or field trip. The trustees would gladly have exchanged with Hamilton or the College of Physicians and Surgeons or the Ashbury Colored Church.

3

Columbia's White Elephant

The sorry expectations which Columbia's trustees entertained about their "Upper Estate," as the land was called to distinguish it from the valuable "Lower Estate" downtown on Park Place, were amply fulfilled. A good year became one which did not require a cash outlay.

"The whole establishment," they complained, "was in a state of dilapidation and decay," but when they made repairs at their own expense, they were no better off.

Denison's lease ran out at the end of 1816, but Columbia could obtain no money rent. The best tenant available was another gardener, Andrew Gentle, who agreed to do no more than keep the grounds and buildings in good order.

The garden was still so attractive that a new Jesuit school decided to locate on the block across Middle Road at Fiftieth Street. The Jesuits were sure that the school would always have a handsome outlook; even if the gardens vanished, it was noted, they would be replaced by a new Columbia campus. (The Jesuit school eventually became the site of St. Patrick's Cathedral.)

Not until 1823, the year before the growing city formally changed the name of Middle Road to Fifth Avenue, was Columbia able to find anyone who would pay money for the use of its Upper Estate. Then John B. Driver, a milkman, agreed to a rent of $125 a year for the twenty acres. Columbia wrote into the lease a provision that the tenant pay any taxes which might be imposed "if the said premises should be deemed taxable or made so during the term." Apparently, the city did not yet regard property in this remote section as worth assessing. Further, in order to preserve the trees and keep the land from being overgrazed, Driver agreed "not to lop, cut, or remove any tree or shrubbery or pasture other than his own cattle."

All this indicates that a very small value indeed was placed on the land. However, visionary men, some of whom were also practical, foresaw a city completely built up from the East River to the Hudson even as far uptown as One Hundredth or One Hundred and tenth streets. In 1811, New York published its first, and by far its most comprehensive, plan for future development. It had been prepared by a group led by Gouverneur Morris, Simon DeWitt, and John Rutherford. They laid out on a map the system of numbered streets and avenues which exist today.

The principal difference between their map and a current one below Central Park is that the land between Third and Seventh avenues and Twenty-third and Thirty-fourth streets was reserved for the old parade ground, already used by the militia. The Elgin Garden is shown as traversed by Forty-eighth, Forty-ninth, Fiftieth, and Fifty-first streets. Middle Road is replaced by Fifth Avenue and the Albany Road, by the Avenue of the Americas.

Before any part of this plan was realized, the legislature released Columbia from the obligation to move to its new property. This was done in an act of 1819 which also relieved the college of the duty to furnish exotic plants to other institutions. It was now possible to sell the land or offer it on a long-term lease, but the twenty acres with improvements were valued at only $7,500, so there was little temptation to sell. One man offered a long term lease, Dr. David Hosack.

The founder, still pursuing his vision of beauty, proposed on three occasions to take the property, but he was becoming cautious in money matters and did not go so far as to promise to pay rent. The trustees politely declined to bind themselves to a lengthy term "unless a source of revenue." In order to cut down maintenance costs, they took advantage of the new act to present to hospitals all the remaining greenhouse plants and a number of ornamental trees and shrubs. Yet as late as 1824 the grounds retained some attraction as a public resort, popularly called Elgin Grove, for a gazetteer of the day reported that it "has as many visitors as the Botanic Garden, chasing pleasure or catching knowledge."

Neither pleasure seekers nor students brought the tenant any profit, and there were better dairy pastures nearer the city. Within two years Driver defaulted on his lease. His successor was David Barnett, a seedsman who seems to have shared the Hosack dream of a market for plants among nature lovers. Barnett rashly promised to pay $500 a year for ten years plus the taxes which finally were levied. Less than a year later he failed; the college realized exactly $118 from a sale of his goods.

The next lease, executed in October, 1828, was the first for a long term and for cash. William Shaw, a farmer with ambitions, had heard talk that Fifth Avenue would be cut through the old parade ground, an improvement which was carried out the next year. He knew that farms in lower Manhattan were yielding to the growth of the city and being divided into building lots. There ought to be a better demand than before for produce from the middle of the island; the Frederick Beinhauer farm directly north of the old Botanic Garden was prospering. So, although Beinhauer's soil was better, Shaw calculated a tidy profit from agriculture while he waited for the land to increase in value. His was the first twenty-one-year lease on the Upper Estate, although he was far from being the Rockefeller of his day.

He paid somewhat less than a Rockefeller price. His rent was to be $400 a year beginning in May 1828. He was to pay taxes and all assessments for improvements, such as streets and grading, if and when realization of the plan of 1811 ever came so far north.

As was to happen to a wealthier tenant just one hundred years later, Shaw found that hardly had he signed the lease than conditions changed. He lived on the land and worked it, but everything was in worse condition than he expected. Most of the soil was too thin or too swampy for crops. The city demanded that he move the eastern stretch of his seven-foot wall because it stuck out twelve feet into Fifth Avenue. In his first four years, he spent more than $5,000 on repairs, for which he had to go into debt. Columbia, recognizing the extent of his hardships, agreed to remit $100 of his rent for each of the next three years.

It was not enough, and Shaw had to give up. One of the men from whom he had borrowed was John Ward, a leading broker and a former president of the Stock Exchange. In November, 1833, Shaw assigned the lease to his creditor.

Then began the earliest negotiations to develop the Upper Estate as a piece of urban realty. Ward, a shrewd, farsighted businessman, proposed to subdivide the twenty acres into city lots under new, longer leases—there would be 256 of these lots by some calculations, 290 by others. Columbia was eager for funds to pay off a rising debt, but its trustees included men just as shrewd as Ward. They held out for a guarantee of at least $46,000 a year. Ward thought this far too much; he was now paying only $350, and several years later he seems to have paid nothing. Neither side would yield, and in the course of the long argument Dr. Hosack's garden finally perished. Before the end of the Shaw lease, the hothouses and greenhouse disappeared; hardly any of the exotic plants, ornamental shrubs, or fruit trees remained.

In 1838, when the property was assessed $121 for improving Fifth Avenue, both Ward and Columbia could see that the complete urbanization of the Upper Estate was only a matter of time. The big question was how much time. After all, for a couple of miles down from this property the avenue was still rural. John Taylor Johnston had a great pillared country residence at Fortieth Street. Christopher Mildeberger's farmhouse at Twenty-third Street was in the process of being converted into a roadhouse known as Colonel Thompson's Madison Cottage, but the land was still farmed. So was the Spingler farm at Fourteenth Street. (More than fifty years later cows still munched grass here, on what was said to be the most expensive pasture in the world, but in the 1840's the owners were just thrifty.) There were still plenty of empty lots all the way from Washington Square to Madison Square. Young men hardly expected to live to see the day when city folk would want to live all the year round way up by the old gardens. The first cross street in the area, Fiftieth, was not opened until 1841.

Soon after that, Ward realized that Columbia never would give anyone favorable terms for developing the whole tract, and he became so disinterested that he neglected to pay the taxes. Twice his lease was sold by the city on this account, and Columbia's books show that the college laid out $1,403.24 to buy the certificates and preserve its clear title to the land.

When the lease finally expired in 1850, nothing of value was left on the ground except a rather run-down dwelling. A standing committee of the Columbia trustees voted to sell the whole Upper Estate to reduce the soaring debt, which now amounted to $68,000, a sum which scared many members. But the full board rejected the idea. It decided to go ahead with the subdivision, much as Ward had planned it, but to prepare the property for leasing in separate lots for one-family dwellings.

Recklessly daring, thought those trustees who wanted to sell. True, Fifth Avenue was becoming fashionable in spots further out than anyone had dreamed a few years earlier. Coventry Waddell's cross between a Gothic castle and an early Tudor villa, the scene of entertainments which even that finicky English visitor Thackeray found pleasant, was way out at Thirty-eighth Street. But surely, the timid trustees argued, no one then living would see the day when anyone of substance would care to live north of Croton Reservoir, which had been completed between Fortieth and Forty-second streets in 1842. The reservoir had become a favorite promenade, with its broad walk on top of the walls. On a good day the saunterers had superb views of Long Island, the Hudson Palisades, and the hills of Westchester. But between the reservoir and the Upper Estate was wasteland or worse. At the corner of Forty-fourth Street, America's first bare-knuckle heavyweight champion, Tom Hyer, ran a little inn and tavern called Ye Olde Willow Cottage. The east side of the avenue from Forty-fourth to Forty-sixth streets was a cattle yard. Hardly desirable neighbors for the fastidious.

Perhaps the fears of some trustees caused the majority's plan to be modified by a renewed proposal that at least part of the property be used for the college itself. The Park Place quarters, cramped enough in 1814, had become intolerable forty years later. Although the Upper Estate was still described in Columbia records as "a few miles from the city," the trustees engaged Richard Upjohn, the architect who had designed new Trinity Church, to draft plans for a building to be erected on the Forty-ninth Street and Fifth Avenue block. Upjohn proposed an imposing edifice with a façade 280 feet long along the Avenue. Estimates for building such a structure were deemed far too high, but this was only one consideration which led the trustees to give up forever the idea of using the site for their college.

They had consumed several years in planning, years which brought them to 1856. Their twenty acres now were worth $550,000; obviously, it was more useful to provide income than a home. Besides, only a block away on Madison Avenue between Forty-ninth and Fiftieth streets, the Deaf and Dumb Asylum was for sale at a price only a fraction of the cost of the Upjohn building. So Columbia moved there in 1857, "temporarily" said the announcement, but it was the home of the college for the next forty years.

To finance this move, the trustees sold sixteen lots at Forty-eighth Street and Fifth Avenue to the Dutch Reformed Church for $40,000. The remainder, after all the streets were laid out, consisted of 272 lots. Considerable discussion of what to do with them ended in a decision to establish a system of leaseholds. The policy then adopted remained in force more than a century later.

The policy is this: Each twenty-one-year lease is renewable for additional twenty-one-year terms with the landlord having the right to buy the buildings at a fair price at the expiration of any term if either the tenant or the college does not renew. The early years of this system added little to Columbia's income. Assessments more than consumed the rents because the Civil War halted most home building, yet streets were improved and much of the land was graded. One of the few leases signed before the war was to Dr. Thomas Ward, a prosperous physician, who built a mansion at Forty-seventh Street and Fifth Avenue. Wits downtown called it "the palace in the wilderness."

The end of the war saw a real estate boom. The pent-up demand for houses was enormous, probably exceeding anything known before or since. Manhattan's most fantastic population explosion took place in the decade before the War Between the States, and it was the culmination of an extremely rapid increase going on for half a century. In the fifty years of Columbia's ownership of the Botanic Garden, the island's population increased about nine times, and more than 40 percent of the growth occurred between 1850 and 1860. Never in the next hundred years, during which Manhattan reached its peak and began to decline, was this rate equaled.

Fewer than 100,000 people had lived on the island in 1810, according to the census. At the end of the War Between the States the estimate was 900,000. Even by the low standards of that day, at least 100,000 of those lacking adequate housing could afford better homes, and they clamored for them.

Once more Columbia's trustees were torn between selling for immediate affluence and holding for a steady income. In 1865 the Collegiate Church of St. Nicholas (Dutch Reformed), built on half the Forty-eighth Street and Fifth Avenue land and sold the other half for $117,000, almost triple the sum paid for their whole tract eight years earlier. The college's trustees thought this was a plain lesson for them, but not all of them got the same message. Some were for selling while the price was high. Others wanted to stick to the policy of leases because the price was high and rents could be raised.

These last prevailed, with the result that by 1869 the last of 272 leases for lots on which 272 homes were to be built was signed. At last Columbia was to receive substantial income from the Upper Estate, enough to compensate for the $150,-000 spent on assessments and improvements.

Dr. Ward was not left long in isolation in his "palace in the wilderness." Mansions marched north along Fifth Avenue in rapid succession and then skipped a few blocks beyond the Upper Estate. Here the Fifth Avenue frontage was soon lined with the four- or five-story, stone-fronted dwellings favored by the architecture of the day, solid but unostentatious. Similar homes were built on the side street lots nearest the avenue; some people preferred these to escape the noisy clatter of horses' hooves and the crack of coachmen's whips.

By 1875 the rest of the property was covered with somewhat more modest houses. For residents who could not afford a horse, transportation downtown was a problem. The stage line on Fifth Avenue operated its brightly painted vehicles—painted with landscapes, Wild West scenes, or famous trotters rather than advertisements—only as far as Forty-second Street.

On the avenue, a second member of the Ward clan, John Quincy Adams Ward, the sculptor whose statue of George Washington still adorns the spot where the first President took the oath of office, built one of the larger homes. He was followed by such eminent New Yorkers as E. L. Godkin, cofounder of the *Nation* and later editor of *The Evening Post,* and William Rhinelander, head of one of the city's oldest and richest Dutch families. Still later came the California millionaire Darius Ogden Mills; Perry Belmont of the famous financial family, and August Heckscher, a member of the newly rich.

Expensive as the several blocks had become, they had a look of deadly monotony. Columbia's leases specified the type of house to be built, the size, and the proportion of the lot it covered. These restrictions were still binding for all except the Fifth Avenue lots when Rockefeller took them over; the condition was eliminated only in his lease.

One brief setback to the prosperity and gentility of the district occurred in the 1870's. Madame Restell, wealthiest and most notorious of the city's abortionists and blackmailers, bought a Fifth Avenue and Fifty-second Street corner as a combination home and place of business. Respectable people, including some of Madame's victims and customers, shunned the neighborhood. But in 1878, the year before the formal opening of St. Patrick's Cathedral in the next block after twenty years of building, the crusading Anthony Comstock managed to have Madame Restell arrested. She killed herself rather than face a court, and real estate resumed its upward progress.

The Fifth Avenue side of Columbia's property, despite its sprinkling of well-known and well-to-do tenants, was not adorned with as many imposing mansions as the blocks just above and below. Fifth Avenue here became the resort of wealth and fashion a little after the Upper Estate was built up. As late as the 1870's, a few farms survived, the neighborhood continued to buy milk, eggs, and vegetables from the Beinhauer farm, operated in its last years by Isaiah Keyser, until William K. Vanderbilt erected there twin chateaux of an elegance which dazzled contemporary writers.

Fashion really singled out the avenue when it became the one north-south street leading to Central Park with neither horsecars nor elevated railroads to discommode the carriages of the Four Hundred. Only then did it begin to replace the "Ladies Mile" of Broadway (from Eighth to Twenty-third streets) as the stylish shopping street—a development which reached as far as Fiftieth Street only in the Twentieth Century. And only then did Vanderbilts, Astors, and Goulds build their ornate mansions. More conservative rich men, including John D. Rockefeller, were content with equally spacious but less ostentatious homes. Toward the end of his life, John D. Rockefeller, Jr., recalled that when he was ten years old, in 1884, his father had bought, just off the avenue on West Fifty-fourth Street, the house of Collis P. Hunting-

The house, garden and stables at No. 4 West 54th Street, home of the John D. Rockefeller family after 1885. This photograph, taken in 1859, shows the site of Rockefeller Center just to the south, mostly rubble-strewn but with a few houses already built.

ton, one of the organizers of the Central Pacific Railroad. He remembered:

It wasn't new then, but we had lived even before that at the Buckingham Hotel at the southeast corner of 50th Street and Fifth Avenue. [It had gone up in 1877 and charged $7 a week for a room.] I remember liking to look at the light pouring through the stained-glass windows of St. Patrick's Cathedral at nightfall.

There weren't many houses in Fifty-fourth Street then. Chauncey Depew was at Number 17. There was an open concrete yard next to my father's house, and in winter it would be flooded and we would all skate on it. When I grew up and married I built my own house across that court. Where our houses were is now the garden of the Museum of Modern Art.

In the beginning the houses were scattered. There were ledges of rock between them and everywhere were great trees. St. Luke's Hospital stood where the University Club is now. The Gurnees lived at the northwest corner of Fifty-sixth. B. Altman later bought their house, and I went there to see the beginning of the great Altman collection. The Kane house at Forty-eighth Street was a very fine limestone structure. Willie K. Vanderbilt and his sister Mrs. Shepherd built houses that occupied the block between Fifty-first and Fifty-second streets.

About that time the land that Columbia had accepted so reluctantly seventy years earlier was valued at $7 million and going up. Even when automobiles began to compete with carriages on the avenue, the solid upper-middleclass atmosphere remained. At the turn of the century and well into the new one, people who ignored the rapidity with which New York always seems to change its desirable residential districts predicted that this would be a neighborhood of fine family homes forever.

The Columbia trustees differed. By 1900, their records reveal, they regarded as inevitable the coming of commerce and modified their Fifth Avenue leases accordingly. But they did not anticipate the vastly greater rents that might be obtained from business for the rest of the land and stubbornly restricted it to one-family residences of the traditional type. This faith was shaken when rents on the avenue soared as much as 600 percent between 1900 and 1920, although side-street prices were steadier.

Meanwhile, Columbia, now a university, was building a big new campus on Morningside Heights. Its move from Madison Avenue was made in 1897; by 1904 it needed money for buildings on the new site. So one block of the Upper Estate between Forty-seventh and Forty-eighth streets was put up for sale. It brought $3 million and reduced the university's holdings to a trifle less than thirteen acres.

Most of the leases on the 199 lots remaining had to be renewed in 1907, a year of panic—or depression, as a more sensitive generation called it. Columbia had to settle for a net of about $300,000 a year, beyond the dreams of trustees of an earlier era but disappointing to a board which had to finance what had become one of the world's great universities.

The years of recovery after 1907 brought little to cheer the owners of this particular land. Fifth Avenue remained desirable. So did the first few houses to the west. But gradually it was noticed that the nearer one approached the clatter of the Sixth Avenue elevated railroad, the shabbier the once genteel brownstones became. Middleclass people unaccountably moved away from this eminently central location. Some of their former homes degenerated into rooming houses. Brass was tarnished, and lace curtains hung limply dingy.

By the time World War I gave way to Prohibition, the neighborhood had deteriorated to a shabbiness which masked a furtive night life. As New York drank and danced and sang its way into the Roaring Twenties, Columbia's once ultrarespectable Upper Estate became a preserve of speakeasies and brothels. A few stubborn families of quality clung to their homes on the eastern fringe of the property. But they and the elegant shops on the avenue were hardly more than a façade which failed to conceal the real nature of most of the houses from anyone who walked through the side streets after dark.

During the Great Boom which led so inexorably to the Great Depression, a discerning observer could spot the better class places of illicit entertainment because they were spick-and-span with polished doorknobs, and clean if heavy drapes hung behind the only windows on the block which seemed to have been washed in a year. Here and there heavy, ostentatious padlocks on the street doors marked the houses shut down by court order after Prohibition raids.

For Columbia, the sole ray of sunshine in this gloom was the fact that most of the leases would expire between 1928 and 1931. With the country entering upon an era proclaimed far and wide as one of perpetual prosperity—thousands of shrewd, capable business and professional men had bet their last dollar on it—the most ambitious plans to reclaim the Upper Estate seemed quite sober.

As important to the future of the Upper Estate as boom and bust in the stock market was the development that many social observers consider the most significant of the decade, the rise of broadcasting. When 1920 opened, not a single transmitter existed to serve the public. In 1922, when the newspapers began to list those stations which had been started, New York had no commercial broadcaster, only an Army Signal Corps job. To find an even half dozen for their list, the papers had to go as far afield as Chicago, Schenectady, and Pittsburgh.

This last, the pioneer of all broadcasting to the public, had begun in April 1920, in a garage where Dr. Frank Conrad of the Westinghouse Company played phonograph records during his radio telephone experiments. To his surprise, amateur hams in the vicinity picked up his signals and began asking him for their favorites.

The next step was a device which David Sarnoff, a former office boy and wireless operator and electrical student, had proposed four years earlier. He wanted to replace headsets, then the only way anyone could hear radio signals, with what he called "a radio telephone receiver . . . designed in the form of a simple 'radio music box' and arranged for several different wavelengths, which could be changeable with the throwing of a single switch or pressing of a single button." The whole family then could listen together and in comfort, he explained; even farmers would be able to tune in on music and lectures from the nearest city. Sarnoff's employers, the

Marconi Wireless Telegraph Company of America, ignored his suggestion. He had to wait for his ideas to materialize when his firm was absorbed in the formation of the Radio Corporation of America after the war.

When New York got a commercial station late in 1922, the American Telephone and Telegraph's WEAF, it started an irresistible trend. WEAF sold advertising; its first commercial advertised a Queens cooperative housing project. By 1926 more than five million radio sets were in use, and in 1927 both the National Broadcasting Company and the Columbia Broadcasting System were functioning as nationwide networks. As the university trustees pondered the future of their Upper Estate, the toy of 1920 became a major industry and—much more important—one which was to prove depression-proof.

The trustees, however, were not thinking of radio, although it would solve their problem, when in January 1928 John W. Tonnele, a vice-president of the William A. White & Company real estate firm suggested that their property might provide a new home for the Metropolitan Opera. It was far more appropriate, he thought, than any of the several sites that the Met had been considering during the last year or so.

4

The Met's Dream

New York's grand opera season in the winter of 1925–26 was
the usual blend of elegant fashion and superior music. Giulio
Gatti-Cazzaza, the flamboyant impresario, was having his
thirteenth and best year since the Metropolitan Opera Company brought him from Milan's La Scala. Excitement among
patrons—and among a public which admired grand opera
only from afar—was divided among the revival of Smetana's
"Bartered Bride," a fortunately noncrippling tumble by
Maria Jeritza, the soprano, from a twenty-foot stage cliff, and
the debut of an incredibly youthful American singer, a
Kansas City girl named Marion Talley, whose appearance in
"Rigoletto" induced such a frenzy of admiration that the
staid old auditorium was literally mobbed and police reserves
were needed to restore order.

The only flaw dimming all this radiance was that auditorium itself. The big block of a building, opened with much fanfare in 1883, was being criticized for inadequacies in both its major roles. Performers were calling it a barn. Spectators objected that it was insufficiently glamorous, especially its location, to set off effectively a woman's jewels, furs, and gowns. Dissatisfaction was especially evident among the parterre boxholders, who in the then organization of the opera were its most influential patrons. However, this group was sharply divided between those who wanted a face-lifting job for the old building and those who preferred a brand new home.

During the first half of this winter of their discontent, the issues were debated chiefly by the directors of the Metropolitan Opera Real Estate Company, which held title to the building. The chairman of its board was Otto H. Kahn, a banker who was widely regarded as the country's most munificent patron of the musical and dramatic arts. On January 12, 1926, he submitted to the directors of both the real estate company and the Opera Company a plan for financing a new home.

He noted that sale of the 1883 structure should bring in a substantial nucleus because the block—bounded by Broadway, Seventh Avenue, Thirty-ninth Street, and Fortieth Street—was an increasingly valuable commercial site. But Kahn also proposed that the Metropolitan Opera finance itself further by including a large office building, the rent from which should meet anticipated operating deficits for culture.

A brief flurry of behind-the-scenes argument among the parterre boxholders was stilled when the president of the Opera Company, R. Fulton Cutting, and its newest director, William K. Vanderbilt, came out for the building project. On January 17, the board voted to go ahead with it, and Otto Kahn was authorized to seek a suitable location.

The three main elements of such a location were proximity to the best theater and shopping districts, good public transportation, and a reasonable land cost, if anything in New York's midtown could be considered reasonable. Furthermore, it would have to be large enough for the office building which the peculiar economics of grand opera in the United States seemed to demand. The peculiarity is that the sale of tickets does not support this particular form of entertainment. The shortness of the season, the great expense of operatic productions, and the limited audience—in 1926, at least, it was not a medium for the masses—combined to guarantee a deficit. The European tradition of a state or royal subsidy was unacceptable in American politics. So the Metropolitan's directors, mostly rich men, had taken the lead in making up the annual shortage. They welcomed a plan that might take them off the hook.

They and the opera were sufficiently newsworthy to bring reports of these doings to the front pages of the New York dailies. Their only rival in that respect was the Park Avenue Baptist Church, also looking for a new home. Its decision to move, publicized in conjunction with the fact that John D. Rockefeller, Jr., was a member of its building committee, made it newsworthy. It was there again when it announced that Rockefeller would give most of the money needed to erect the church on a Riverside Drive site near Grant's Tomb. His name was not mentioned in the opera stories.

The Kahn committee quietly assembled a plot on Fifty-seventh Street between Eighth and Ninth avenues, then a neighborhood of medium-priced stores, small offices, and apartments. The necessary negotiations took months. In order to prevent the asking price of land from soaring astronomically, it was essential that the identity of the potential buyer be concealed. But options were obtained, and the Metropolitan's architect went to work on plans. He was Benjamin Wistar Morris, a leader of his profession, and his design for the new opera house was in the modern tradition, blending well enough with an accompanying twelve-story office structure. He had hardly completed preliminary sketches than the Kahn committee had second thoughts about the Fifty-seventh Street plot. It was small; opera house and office building would both be cramped on it. It was abandoned, and Morris went to Europe to look at the way opera was housed there—by this time it was early summer in 1927.

He came back fired with a far more ambitious idea than even the princely Otto Kahn had dreamed. He wanted not only a larger opera house than his previous version but he proposed to build into it a number of music studios and to set it in a spacious plaza with trees, shrubs and flowers, fountains, and a pool. Above would tower a skyscraper rivaling the tallest in the city—he explained that it would have to be that big if the rents were to carry the extra land he envisaged for the plaza and the additional space for studios. Two sites seemed possible, one on Broadway between Sixty-second and Sixty-third streets, the other on Columbus Circle at the southwest corner of Central Park. Both were a little farther from the best shopping streets than the opera directors desired.

That objection might have been overcome, but as Morris reviewed his new plans, neither he nor the directors were quite satisfied. The office building had to be so big that it must completely dominate the landscape, overwhelming both the opera house and the plaza. Morris' architectural ingenuity could offer no solution to this problem; there simply was not enough land in either site to work with effectively.

Then a way out seemed to open. Since the Met's decision to move was about two years old, it was hardly any secret in the real estate world. One of the men who knew about it was John Tonnele whose firm had been engaged by Columbia to find tenants to improve the Upper Estate as the leases expired. In January 1928, when he suggested the possibility of a development that would include the opera, the university's trustees thought so well of it they agreed to sell as much of the land to the Met as it would need, although they preferred to retain ownership of all.

Both Cutting and Morris were also enthusiastic. The architect wrote that the idea "fathered my thought," and he put the thought on paper in the form of a sketch which included not only the spacious plaza and imposing opera house of his earlier plans, but no fewer than seven other buildings spaced around the three blocks of the Columbia property. Three of them were skyscrapers, and all were linked one story above the ground by a broad promenade lined with shops. The plaza with its gardens and fountains occupied the center of the property.

At this stage the opera's directors were confident of being able to sell their old house for $12 million or a little more. The estimate for building a new one was $8.5 million. This would leave at least $3.5 million to buy land. But Columbia wanted $6 million for the portion earmarked on Morris' sketch for the opera and plaza, a reasonable price as the market then rated, but calling for a little more financial muscle than the Met boasted.

To whip up interest, some of the most eminent directors gave a dinner at the Metropolitan Club in May to let Morris expound his plans and spark formation of a syndicate to buy the plaza site as a gift to the city. Among the guests was the Rockefeller public relations adviser, Ivy Lee, who reported on the meeting to Colonel Arthur Woods of the Rockefeller staff.

"The plan commended itself to me as a highly important civic improvement," Rockefeller said later, "and I agreed to participate in it."

Almost before he knew it, he was doing more. The syndicate of dinner guests fizzled out in talk, but Rockefeller's interest grew, and he began to consider the possibility of a much larger venture. He consulted five real estate experts independently, asking each to estimate what, leaving out the land needed for opera house and plaza, he should be able to realize on subleases to commercial interests which would erect their own buildings along the lines of Morris' plan. The lowest estimate of his income from such a project was $3,156,-000; the highest, $5,580,000. All five, he recalled some years afterward, "pronounced the project a sound one and good business."

On the basis of this advice, Rockefeller opened his own negotiations with Columbia. In August the terms of a mutually acceptable agreement were embodied in a memorandum. It gave Rockefeller an option to buy a strip about five hundred feet wide running from Forty-ninth Street to Fiftieth Street on the west side of the property for $6 million and pay $3.3 million a year for a lease on the rest. The lease was to be for twenty-four years with options for three renewals of twenty-one years each.

The optioned part was subject to these conditions: Rockefeller would resell three fifths of the plot to the Metropolitan Opera Company for $3.6 million and use the rest for "an open square." Then followed detailed provision for recapturing the land and adding it to the leased part for extra rent if the opera house was not built. Other clauses required the lessee to pay taxes and provided for deductions from his rent on lots which still had leases outstanding.

Such deals are seldom kept entirely secret, and the day after this memorandum was drafted, *The Herald Tribune* had an exclusive but slightly exaggerated story to the effect that Rockefeller had acquired an option to buy the property for forty or fifty million dollars. Four months later *The New York Times* went its rival one better and announced that he *had* bought it, and for $100 million. In point of fact, the first would have been a bargain; the second, excessive. The best guess of real estate men at the time was that the Upper Estate was worth $62 million.

Of course Rockefeller had not really been as impulsive as these articles made him seem. What he had done after consulting his own real estate experts was to inquire of John R. Todd, the hard-headed but imaginative head of the Todd, Robertson, Todd Engineering Corporation, how he would develop such a property. Todd, a lawyer by profession, had an almost intuitive grasp of urban construction problems and tempered his knowledge and experience with a streak of aestheticism. He had believed that a plan to finance grand opera with commercial rentals carried the seeds of trouble, both for the commercial sponsors and for the cultural enterprise. He thought the two were properly separated in the present proposal as indicated in the memorandum.

To make clear what he had in mind, Todd suggested that an architect he admired, L. Andrew Reinhard, design a tentative plan for the development. Reinhard and his partner Henry Hofmeister flung themselves into this work over the Labor Day weekend and came up with the second sketch of how Columbia's Upper Estate might look. In the annals of Rockefeller Center the result is still known as the "Labor Day scheme." Experts primarily in the subdividing of office space within an existing structure, Reinhard and Hofmeister included only one office building in their design for the three blocks, but they proposed two hotels, one of thirty-five stories and the other of thirty-seven. They left the opera site and plaza more or less as Morris had indicated them and suggested low buildings to flank the opera house north and south.

A few weeks later, on October 1, the actual formal agreement embodying in legal language the terms of the August memorandum was signed and it was from that date that the lease would run. The option to purchase the opera and plaza sites was to be open throughout the first term of the lease. An added feature was that while Rockefeller might assign his rights to the corporation he was setting up for the purpose, but to no one else, he was to remain personally and individually liable for carrying it out. The corporation, wholly owned by Rockefeller, was called the Metropolitan Square Corporation, and Colonel Woods became its first President.

Shortly thereafter Rockefeller left for a trip to Egypt, so he was unavailable for inquisition by the reporters when on January 22, 1929, President Nicholas Murray Butler of Columbia issued a public announcement of the lease, the amount of rent, and its general purpose. (Through 1965 the rent has totalled $130,912,636.) While the Columbia statement seemed to take it for granted that the new opera house would be located here, a Rockefeller spokesman was less specific, expressing it cautiously as a hope.

Perhaps it was that caution which led to some vagueness in the explanation of what was afoot. *The New York Times* for one got the impression that the *Place de l'Opera* in Paris was to be the model, with high-priced shops facing a Capitol of Music across some sort of open square, but with a New World refinement. The cafés where shoppers could refresh themselves while they watched the traffic on Fifth Avenue and the side streets were to be on an elevated promenade.

"I leased these three blocks," Rockefeller was to remember, "never thinking for a moment but that I could shortly sublet the remaining property to various organizations which, without further investment on my part, would develop and finance their own building programs as the opera proposed to do."

From about this time forward, the arrangement and size of the other buildings occupied an increasingly large proportion

Wallace K. Harrison's first sketch of the Metropolitan Opera project, drawn in the early spring of 1929. The opera house, designed for the western side of what is now Rockefeller Center, is the massive structure in the background. The colonnaded arcades are perhaps one reason *The New York Times* thought the *Place de l'Opera* in Paris was the model.

of his and his advisers' attention, but the opera house remained as the center of all the plans. It was the starting point for every one of the hundreds of designs which were sketched by a platoon of architects during the rest of the year.

Significantly, however, it was the Metropolitan Square Corporation and not the Opera Company that appointed and supervised and paid the architects. In the best tradition of the patron of arts, the corporation invited several people whose firms already had been consulted to submit designs with a deadline in May. The ones still remembered were those submitted by Raymond M. Hood and Wallace K. Harrison. Although neither plan played much part in the future development of the project, even while the opera remained its major feature, these two men were to have more influence upon the final version than any others, although the contributions of many are easily discernible.

Hood at this time was in his early fifties, one of the most highly respected members of his profession. He had only recently become fully committed to what his biographer has called the revolutionary new style of those called "modernists." He had leaped into the forefront of American architects by winning first prize and the commission for the Chicago Tribune Building, a highly controversial and widely admired structure which has since been termed "one of the turning points in the history of American twentieth-century architecture." (The turning point in his career, too, for he and his wife had sacrificed a great deal to maintain the integrity of his ideas and were deeply in debt. One of the cheeriest stories in architecture is that of Mrs. Hood riding around New York in a taxicab with the $50,000 prize check in her hand to show to all the creditors before she deposited it.)

Hood had created almost as much of a stir with the American Radiator Building in New York, a tall, narrow shaft of black brick crowned with golden terra cotta. He had just finished the even more revolutionary Beaux Arts Apartments and, what many think is his masterpiece, the Daily News Building on Forty-second Street, which achieved more grace and style with the setbacks required by zoning laws than had previously been thought possible.

Harrison, nearly twenty years Hood's junior, had been committed even longer to America's architectural revolution. He had nothing like Hood's achievements to his credit at yet, but he had recently become the junior partner of a much better known member of the profession, Harvey Wiley Corbett. No man held more firmly than Harrison to the principle that in the design of a major architectural enterprise, such as a large office building, the form should grow out of the nature of the work to be done in it. He argued that the needs of the people who would do the work ought to be an

architect's first consideration. He had definitely and deci-
sively parted from the school which held that the building
should be beautiful, and then the people could be stuffed
into it somehow.

Throughout the summer of 1929 there were ardent but
inconclusive discussions, some of them at the Rockefeller
summer home, about the nature of the designs. Decision was
blocked by the sheer size and audacity of the project. Never
before had architects, engineers, and builders been called
upon to plan a single private development of what must be at
least ten or a dozen major buildings—it turned out to be
fourteen for this first phase. The concept of such a veritable
city of skyscrapers and subsidiary structures had never before
been applied to commercial real estate. The only comparable
projects had been some of the vast public or state or church
ventures in Europe in the distant past.

Small wonder, then, that the men who had to grapple with
the problems, many of which were magnified in geometric
proportion by the scope of the project, took a lot of time—
discussed, debated, sketched, and discarded. They were all
fully aware that theirs was an opportunity to create an architectural complex such as the world had never seen. They
were understandably cautious because there were no prece-
dents to guide them on some points, and yet it was essential
to foresee and provide for almost unpredictable difficulties.

The talk culminated in October, just as the stock market
began to break badly, in the appointment of two of John
Todd's firms to be managers of the project. This was followed
in a few weeks by the organization of an architectural group
of which the chief members were Morris of the Opera Company, Ray Hood, Corbett, Harrison, Reinhard, and Hofmeister. They promptly began to develop plot plans based
upon the May designs plus the "Labor Day scheme" plus
suggestions which had been made since.

They were mercifully spared the necessity for too much

detail. During all this discussion, it was taken for granted that the actual construction costs would be spread widely. The Met would pay for its own auditorium and studios from the proceeds of the old house. The plaza in front of it was to be the Rockefeller contribution: he would pay for it and present it to the city. The rest of the land would be subleased to private individuals or corporations who would erect their own buildings in conformity with the over-all design. Under this arrangement, merchants would have put up the department stores—two were indicated on most of the plans—hotel men, the hotels and commercial developers, the office buildings. But as yet no businessmen in any of these categories had been approached.

Meanwhile, the new managers of the project had inherited some unexpected difficulties in getting control of all the 229 existing structures on the estate. The eighteen tenants who still had leases with years to run and a few of the others, too, had larger ideas about the value of their holdings than had been anticipated. The original estimate to buy them off had been $600,000. Twice that figure now was not enough. Partly on this account negotiations with the Metropolitan Opera Company, which President Butler of Columbia had seemed to think were to be a mere formality in January, ran into snags in October.

November, however, was the critical month. As the stock market plummetted down—the biggest single break in history came on October 29—the demands of leaseholders rose as if they hoped to recoup in the Upper Estate their losses on Wall Street. They were holding out for a total of $1,250,000 at just the time that the directors of the opera were acutely aware of the unlikelihood they would be able to sell their Broadway-Seventh Avenue site for anything like the cost of putting up a new building, let alone having something left over to buy leases. They proposed that Rockefeller pay half the cost of this. When he rejected the request because he thought his contribution of $2.4 million for the plaza site was enough for one man, they suggested he buy the opera site too and sublet it to them. He refused this one on the ground that if the opera ran into financial difficulties he did not want, as the landlord, to be the one blamed for killing it.

Three years of hopes and dreams which had seemed so close to fulfillment ended on this sorrowful note. The decision was cloaked in the soothing verbiage of a joint statement issued by the Metropolitan and Rockefeller. This document neatly side-stepped any hint that mere money was a matter of consequence to either of the parties. It would not have been good form for the distinguished gentlemen of the Opera's Board to confess their company's poverty. In those days of desperate reassurances that all was well with the national economy, the truth about the Met's financial positon might have been disillusioning. Apparently there was a lingering belief that somewhere in the country people still had illusions about the stability of the market.

At any rate, the public announcement issued on Thursday, December 4, said obscurely that it had been "impossible to overcome certain difficulties." Since it was considered necessary to avoid mention of the most important of these, the stubborn brownstone tenants were cited as the specific insuperable obstacles. The statement asserted without explanation that in order to participate in the project on the Columbia property, the Opera Company had to be guaranteed possession of a new home in time for opening night in 1931. (Thirty-five years later they have it a mile away at Lincoln Center.) The Metropolitan Square Corporation was not able to give such a guarantee, it was added, because there was no certainty of being able to acquire the outstanding leases promptly.

The statement closed with a brisk paragraph declaring that

Rockefeller was going ahead with the development of the property anyway. Two days later came the entry in the Metropolitan Square Corporation's minutes about "a commercial center as beautiful as possible consistent with the maximum income that could be developed." Long afterward the man responsible for that decision explained:

Thus it came about that with the depression underway and values falling rapidly, I found myself committed to Columbia for a long-term lease, wholly without the support of the enterprise by which and around which the whole development had been planned.

Moreover, the general financial situation was so steadily getting worse that there was no possibility of subletting unimproved, as contemplated, any portion of the area . . . There were only two courses open to me. One, to abandon the entire development. The other, to go forward with it in the definite knowledge that I myself would have to build and finance it alone without the immense impetus that the new opera house would have given and with no escape from the fact that under the changed conditions it would be necessary to improve all the land in order to lease it, thus involving immense capital outlays never contemplated. I chose the latter course.

The choice was made with the further knowledge that estimates of the "capital outlays" ran to about $200 million. But even this was perhaps less of a cause for hesitation than the potential dynamite contained in the twofold objective of beauty and profit, a danger of which Rockefeller was not heedless.

He was anything but a novice in dealing with New York real estate. One of his companies had been formed to erect model tenements—some of them in Harlem are considered superior models forty years later. Another had bought and sold city property involving millions. The negotiations for the new Riverside Church had occupied much of his attention.

With this background, he could hardly fail to realize that in a commercial real estate enterprise of unexampled magnitude, such as he was contemplating, some sharp conflicts were bound to develop. The most obvious and perhaps the most serious were those inherent in human nature. It would be inevitable that some of his subordinates would think his statement's governing phrase was "as beautiful as possible." Others would give obeisance to "the maximum income that could be developed."

In the long run, the success of the venture, from his own standpoint, would depend upon the way in which he as the ultimate authority could reconcile the two. He was able to preserve an easy impartiality because in his own mind there was no conflict. He saw no contradiction in the two parts of his directive. That other men might have trouble grasping so comprehensive a view did not bother him much, for he understood them without yielding his principles to theirs. His son Nelson remembers that the older man's ideal was a combined business and cultural center which "considers itself a civic institution," but in which neither business nor culture necessarily domineered over the other.

Rockefeller supposed that businessmen had their civic obligations like everybody else. He was not at all outraged by the idea that beauty could serve commerce. So with these points comfortably harmonized in his own thinking, however antagonistic they might seem to others, he moved with characteristic serenity into the new situation imposed upon him by the Opera Company's withdrawal and the deepening economic depression.

5
Down to Earth

A student of architecture, writing in 1942, described the Rockefeller directive as having resulted in a group of fourteen buildings which were unique in America because they had been developed at different times for various purposes but in harmony with a definite scheme.

"In this sense," he added, "it is similar in architectural concept to the *Forum Romanum,* the Church of St. Peter's at Rome, or the Louvre Museum in Paris."

It is doubtful that the architects actually at work in 1930 would have made any such comparison. They were too anxiously concerned with special problems of the modern age. They were designing a commercial complex in which men and women would have to work and through which more people would move every day than had lived in Rome or Paris when St. Peter's and the Louvre were new. Aesthetes may ignore these factors in judging architecture—in fact they often do—but the first question for the men who must live with the result is how well it serves human needs. For them and for the community as a whole even the criteria of beauty and profit play second fiddle.

The bigger the project, the more this is so, and the one soon to be known as Rockefeller Center was the biggest of its kind that men had yet attempted. In such an undertaking the difficulties of arranging passage for pedestrians and wheeled vehicles are very different in nature and degree from any confronted by architects of earlier centuries. Movement is up and down in elevators as well as horizontally along streets and promenades and corridors. The means for bringing in supplies needed by hundreds of varied businesses with thousands of employees must be provided, but out of the way and mostly out of sight of the ordinary passengers. These have to be able to get in and out morning, noon, and night without unbearable traffic jams at unforeseen bottlenecks. Light and air and space per person are more important considerations for working quarters than most past generations thought them to be.

Of course, some guides to the best solutions of these problems existed. Surveys of the traffic that develops in and around office buildings could be made and the experience of others, studied. It was possible, therefore, to estimate the number of people, trucks, cars, and handcarts that would have to be accommodated at various times. It was possible to calculate how many elevators of a certain size moving at a certain speed would be needed to serve each floor and bank of floors. The Empire State Building, just completed, was a salutary example. Hood had worked out some of the problems successfully in the Daily News Building.

The Center's architects had the complicating new factor of interchange between a group of buildings, which had not confronted the designers of single office structures, hotels, or department stores. These questions took up a great deal of the time of the men who had been established in large drafting offices in the Graybar Building next to Grand Central Station. About thirty architects plus 120 draftsmen, clerks, and others were employed, the chiefs remaining the same except for the withdrawal of Morris after the opera was no longer a participant. At various times in the next few years the arrangements with the architects were revised, but the major figures were those already involved.

Within a month of the December 6 decision each of these gentlemen had produced drawings with fundamentally new arrangements of line and elevation. The removal of the opera as the central element led each to place the tallest towers of the major building toward Sixth Avenue, with lower structures fronting on Fifth. Each design called for new streets, although on some these were parallel with existing thoroughfares and on some they appeared as diagonals. Each of the designs also set aside space for a plaza and included a promenade with shops one floor above ground level with arcades and bridges spanning the streets to connect the various buildings.

The first casualty of the architectural concept was the elevated promenade. Management—apparently John Todd's influence on this point was decisive—decided the cost would be prohibitive. The other principal difference between these drawings and what one now sees was that the designs offered neatly, precisely balanced shapes and masses while the uses to which the buildings were to be put, and second thoughts on over-all effects, led to actual construction without so much regard for regularity.

To compensate for this, long before the architects began to reconcile their early concepts with the decisions of management, they were told to include in their plans the strip of land fronting on Sixth Avenue that Columbia did not own. Even before the opera withdrew, Rockefeller and his advisers were exploring the purchase of these lots. Taking elaborate precautions to avoid betraying the identity of the purchaser— a new corporation, a new set of agents and brokers, etc.—all but two of the lots were acquired between the late summer of 1929 and the fall of 1930. The sum needed, which Rockefeller advanced to the new company, was $5,365,000.

This acquisition, especially that in the block between Forty-ninth and Fiftieth streets, set both management and the architects free to get down to the brass tacks of planning for specific tenants. It was important because just at this time the negotiations which determined not only the principal tenant but much of the nature of the whole project were in process. They sprang partly from a conversation between an architect and a banker, partly from a far-reaching antitrust action which involved no one connected with Rockefeller Center.

The architect was Wallace Harrison, who happened during the winter of 1929–30 to have lunch with Julian and Narcissa Street, son-in-law and daughter of Frank Vanderlip, former president of the National City Bank, and the conversation turned, naturally enough, to the plans on which Harrison was working. There had been talk of various industries which might replace the opera as the core of the project, and the young giant called radio had been one. The Philharmonic had been another, but nothing came of that except some drawings.

When Narcissa Street told her father of this, Vanderlip had a practical suggestion for Harrison. He said the Radio Corporation of America, by far the largest company in the field, might be interested. It turned out that his uncle, Edward Harden, an RCA director who was chairman of the company's real estate committee, could confirm this.

Without some such tip, it is unlikely that RCA would have been considered a candidate for the center. It had a big, brand new building of its own only a couple of blocks away, at Lexington Avenue and Fifty-first Street. However, it was drifting into a peculiar situation, understood at this time only by a few insiders, in which it would be orphaned by the five big companies which had given birth to it only a decade before. The five were General Electric, Western Electric, American Telephone and Telegraph, Westinghouse, and United Fruit. They were the owners of virtually all the radio patents that mattered, and during World War I they had pooled them so successfully for the benefit of the government that after the war the government asked them to keep the pool alive by organizing RCA as a company they would own jointly. The key man in that reorganization was Owen D. Young, chairman of General Electric, and he remained the most potent individual in the affairs of the RCA.

At the time it was presumed that the major business of the firm would be competition with the telegraph and cable companies. Entertainment and broadcasting into homes entered no one's mind, except perhaps for Sarnoff, who was not getting much attention on this point. But ten years later, with Sarnoff as president, RCA dominated the new radio business through its subsidiary, National Broadcasting Company, which owned the two largest nationwide networks. RCA was also the parent of RCA Victor, leading manufacturer of phonographs and records, and Radio-Keith-Orpheum, one of the major movie producing, distributing, and exhibiting companies. The government was beginning to suggest that it was too much for the leading electrical firms (United Fruit was hardly that, but had been included because of some patents it owned) to control such a big user of their products. Young, who agreed, was preparing to accept a decree which would separate all five from RCA as soon as a suit should be filed, and he was anticipating a few problems connected with the split. One of them was a debt of several million dollars which RCA owed to General Electric.

RCA was one of the few big corporations to which some of the boom's glamour still clung, but not because of any large money resources. Although at the peak of the market its stock had been quoted at 573¾, it had never paid a dividend and could lay its hands on cash for only a small fraction of its debt. But Young knew that his colleague, Gerard Swope, president of General Electric, wanted to move the company's headquarters uptown, out of the financial district with all its unfortunate connotations for consumers. Talks which ended with General Electric allowing RCA $7 million for the Lexington Avenue building were begun.

Wallace Harrison remembers that it was Young who listened to Vanderlip, gazing abstractedly out of his window at 120 Broadway as if he really did not altogether approve, a characteristic pose. He came to life when his visitor had finished. He swung around briskly and exclaimed energetically, "Let's go see Sarnoff and Mr. Rockefeller."

They did, and from that point negotiations proceeded with RCA and the Rockefeller managers discussing a deal involving no fewer than four theaters and large parts of two office buildings—a million square feet of office space was mentioned. The architects had a field day for a while; for all the firmness with which they defended their various opinions, they reached conclusions more readily than might be expected, and more readily than they themselves ever did again with other colleagues on other projects. One reason was that Rockefeller knew how to handle them. The other, which had more effect a little later, was their vivid awareness that this was about the only architectural job of consequence in New York. It kept them not only on their toes but out of each other's hair.

Rockefeller's way with them was a reflection of his personality and his absorbing interest in what they were doing. In a way he was getting his money's worth out of his unpremeditated dive into urban real estate, for details of design and building fascinated him. In 1930 and the following several years he indulged his taste to the full. As chairman of the building committee of Riverside Church he had been meeting to consider its construction details once a week for months and months—it opened on October 5, 1930. He was in the early stages of the restoration of Colonial Williamsburg, an enterprise at least as ambitious as the Center if not quite so expensive.

If it was possible to have a surfeit of drawings, plans, and blueprints, this should have been it. But Rockefeller enjoyed it all and in the offices at the Graybar Building he served so ably as a moderator, conciliator, and boss that some of his architects said later that they had pooled their ideas under his chairmanship with unexampled success. If he was, as someone described him, "living knee deep in blueprints," it was a happy life. For years he had carried a four-foot rule in his hip pocket. Now it was his hallmark and symbol of authority. He was always whipping it out to make a point or to have one explained.

"He was immersed in the kind of detail he loved," says his biographer Raymond Fosdick.

"You had to watch your step with him," Harrison says, "because he would pull out his ruler and check on you."

For purposes of the RCA negotiations, his architects produced in March, 1930, a plan for four theaters on Sixth Avenue, a towering RCA building where it actually stands, and three other office buildings, including a strange elliptical structure smack in the center of the Fifth Avenue frontage.

"And was that ridiculous!" exclaims Harrison as he looks back at those days which strike even him as a little mad,

John D. Rockefeller, Jr. at his desk in Rockefeller Center in 1937, applying his four-foot rule to a set of blueprints. "You had to watch your step with him." (Photograph courtesy of *Life* magazine.)

fabulous, and yet productive. "How did they expect people to get around that big oval building to the even bigger one in back of it?"

His anguish was not reflected in the negotiation chamber, for the design was good enough to sew up RCA's agreement, signed on June 4, 1930. The company undertook to pay as rent for four theaters (two of which might be dropped) and the space to be occupied in two office buildings the sum of $4,250,000 a year. (It probably induces a state of nostalgia in the company's disbursing office to recall that the office rent was calculated at $2.75 a square foot. Tenants who pay triple that for comparable space in 1965 are considered to be getting a bargain.)

The agreement gave the lessee the right to name the thea-

The first publicly displayed plaster model of what Rockefeller Center might become, exhibited March 5, 1931. The much-reviled "pillbox" was actually an oval, being slightly distorted in perspective here.

ters, the two buildings in which its headquarters were to be housed, and that whole entertainment section of the development. It is in accordance with this clause that "Radio City" was coined; it applies properly only to the western side of Rockefeller Center. Another clause gave NBC the right to construct studios—elaborate specifications were attached— even to television accommodations if and when that unlikely experimental medium might in the remote future reach a marketable stage. Finally, the Center agreed that no other tenant than NBC should have the right to engage in the business of broadcasting.

The actual leases embodying the terms of the agreement were signed with some ceremony on October 29, 1931. Meanwhile, the plans and even the construction proceeded side by side with supplementary and complementary designs for tenants who never materialized, and then finally for some who did. Yet much of the design had to be tentative, even when the needs of RCA were believed to be settled.

The huge NBC studios, for example, with no supporting internal walls, and the special traffic problem of broadcasters who have to have three separate arrangements for performers, other workers, and the public, caused some modifications most of which Hood worked out. He had designed the smaller NBC studios at 711 Fifth Avenue and knew more about them than any of the other architects. He knew so much that his foresight was largely responsible for the fact that after more than thirty years and a whole series of technical broadcasting revolutions they are still in use.

One of the summer plans which management liked provided for all four of the new tenant's theaters and a concert hall or opera house besides, all grouped around three sides of a large central plaza, while a tall, massive department store adorned one of the Fifth Avenue corners.

Shortly thereafter, Harrison, supported by Hood, won a tactical victory. He likes to embody finished designs in three-dimensional models rather than drawings. He argues that the model makes it possible to see what the building will really look like all around, not just from the front. He thinks it is especially important in a skyscraper, because it permits thorough understanding of exactly what happens when service areas are dropped out as the upper floors are reached. If the architect is preoccupied with one aspect, he can go wrong on the space.

Harrison doesn't remember being very enthusiastic about the first Rockefeller Center model even so, because it featured the oval building on Fifth Avenue. This had been inserted in the first place to suit a prospective banking tenant. By the time the model was completed, the bank had bowed out of the picture. But there was such keen public curiosity about the plans that the management decided to unveil its pretty little plaster toy even if the oval had been scrapped. So they went ahead with the show on March 5, 1931, in the Graybar Building, and reaped a reward of scorn and ridicule.

"Radio City is ugly. Its exterior is revoltingly dull and dreary," *The Herald Tribune* declared.

"Never can such universal condemnation have been visited upon a great artistic project as that which has been the lot of the suggested buildings for Radio City." *The New York Times* editorialized and went on to complain of "architectural aberrations and monstrosities."

"Pill box" was almost the kindest remark in the press. Another critic thought it resembled a gas house and still another was reminded of "a jeweled powder box on a dressing table." Less caustic objections, but only slightly less, were made about the other dominant structure, the RCA Building, which in this plan was a seventy-story slab, the first of this kind to be a real skyscraper. Much too high was the general opinion of the critics.

While the elliptical motif was dropped forever, the adverse comments did not deter either architects or management from going ahead with the RCA Building substantially as shown in the model. They kept offices out of the top four floors, but not to meet criticism. Servicing them would have added to the costs out of all proportion to the rentable space gained, so this area was left to house machinery. In fact, sixty-six stories were not strictly the most economical. Forty-five is the optimum for skyscrapers in this setting when building and operating costs are balanced coldly against potential rents. But taller ones have prestige and visual value, and although the Center never exceeded the optimum again, its management never regretted this splurge.

The architectural philosophy which really determined the

finished designs has been succinctly put by Harrison as "the study first of all of the human being." In amplification, he says:

We started from a single person and added one person to another, and one floor to another, deciding what was the proper light, proper height, proper distance from the elevator. You have to be free to change your concept, not once, not twice, but many times. Still, you don't change after the building begins; you should make all your mistakes on paper. We had all kinds of different ideas on the drawing board and in our models—different tops on the RCA Building, different windows, different walls. I remember one design for an exterior wall was like a splendid tapestry of brick and tile and stone. It was beautiful—only there was no way to build it.

In the long run, Harrison and Hood got more of their ideas across than the others, partly because they thought alike. Harrison remembers only one serious difference between them, and this one was a hard-fought struggle. It concerned the front of the RCA Building. Hood proposed a Rockefeller Plaza entrance with the arches, as is there now. Harrison wanted the façade to rise straight up from the street without any interruptions.

"Ray won," he says, "and now I think he was right. On everything else, though, we stuck together."

Apparently the pair got into plenty of arguments that tested their solidarity. With three of the leading firms in town represented, there was never any shortage of opinions. All the men involved were or proved themselves later to be achievers, and "every one of us had a conceit as big as Frank Lloyd Wright's," Harrison puts it. This was one reason for resorting to models rather than just drawings, since models made the disputed points clearer. Harrison, Hofmeister, and Reinhard were in the office all day every day, having given up all other work. Hood was there every morning and often

Raymond Hood (left) and Wallace K. Harrison with one of their
models early in 1932. Harrison's hand seems to be resting on the
Eastern Air Lines Building, although that edifice was not yet
planned. The model was made to show La Maison Francaise
(left) and the British Empire Building with the RCA Building
rising behind them.

in the afternoon as well, working himself to death, Harrison
thinks—indeed, Hood did die in 1934. Corbett was active in
the early stages and André Fouilhoux, Hood's partner, in the
later ones.

When the architects got down to their final blueprints, the
outline of the RCA Building was determined as much by the
angle of the sun in the latitude of New York as anything else.

The chief factor governing the size and spacing of windows was flexibility in subdividing the space behind them, while preserving adequate light all over. The setbacks were dictated by the lighting, internal traffic and service problems, not by the city building regulations. The size of the windows led to a somewhat higher ceiling than was then, or is now, usual. It could be justified by citing one of Rockefeller's favorite phrases, "the last 5 percent." He held that the mere one-twentieth extra was worth it to get top quality.

The principal architectural decision really was that the sort of work done in offices prescribed all working space within twenty-seven feet of an outside wall. This is as far as daylight reaches in New York during most working hours of most working days. The interior of the building beyond that could contain elevators, washrooms, closets for storage, plumbing, and assorted service needs. A constant twenty-seven-foot ring of usable space around a core that shrinks as one ascends was a must only for the office building; department stores or lofts or hotels would be quite different, because their use of space would not depend so much on daylight.

Then the windows were spaced five feet apart so that when a tenant wanted to put up partitions he would not be restricted to the edges of those windows as he is in an all-steel and glass building. When there is hardly any space between panes, the interior arrangement is relatively inflexible because no one wants to run a divider at right angles to the middle of a window.

The setbacks were placed in accordance with the decreased need for elevator shafts, emergency stairs, and other utilities. When the elevators serving the lowest floors ended, the setback began so that the outer walls always remained twenty-seven feet from the core on all four sides. As each bank of elevators was dropped off, another setback appeared.

It all seems obviously desirable, although it is not always the architectural practice. The dimensions have proved so sound, however, that they are followed to this day. An award-winning CBS Building, across the street on the now Avenue of the Americas from Rockefeller Center and finished as this book went to press, has made much of its thirty-five feet of uninterrupted space between the core and outer walls—this includes corridor space. A critic praised its five-foot windows five feet apart so "you will be able to move around office partitions at will without making structural changes."

In the working and reworking of the Rockefeller Center designs, the idea of an elevated shopping promenade was replaced by schemes for shops in a lower concourse. To provide access to them, the architects devised a sunken plaza with flowers and shrubs and splashing fountains. This feature was retained through all the future vicissitudes of planning, but never fulfilled its original purpose. Instead, it was used for ice skating in winter and outdoor dining and dancing in summer. Architects may bewail the failure to serve any more practical function in a commercial complex, but the sunken plaza remains one of the most popular of Rockefeller Center's attractions.

In justice to the architects, it must be added that they were not simply doodling when they dreamed up this feature to go below ground level. The rumbling eyesore of the Sixth Avenue Elevated was supposed to be replaced by a subway about the time these new buildings would be completed. But the Depression and later municipal financial difficulties delayed the project so long that the Center was finished—at least the first phase of it—long before there was any subway for people using the sunken plaza to enter.

Another feature inserted in the plans at this stage and never changed again was the private street running through the plot from north to south, eventually named Rockefeller Plaza. Begining even before any buildings were completed, an annual ceremony to preserve Columbia's right of ownership of the strip occupied by the street was held. This consists of closing the street to all traffic, even pedestrian, one day a year—a Sunday in July is chosen as interfering least with tenants and visitors. If this formality should be skipped, the public might eventually acquire a permanent right of way here. A much more frequently noticed mark of the university's ownership is a brass strip set into the pavement to outline the boundaries of Columbia's Upper Estate.

By the time the architects had advanced this far, the businessmen were facing up to the expense. Todd and his associates estimated that the buildings would cost $125 million of which a bit more than half could be borrowed from the Metropolitan Life Insurance Company on mortgage bonds, it was determined after considerable negotiation. A Todd memorandum dated March 27, 1931, starts off: "65 at 5 . . . Amortization, etc. to be arranged." And at the end he wrote: "Completion of building to be guaranteed by Mr. David."

This meant that Metropolitan Life would lend $65 million at 5 percent ($45 million was actually borrowed) if Rockefeller would be as personally responsible for the costs of construction as he was for the Columbia lease. The "Mr. David" concealed his identity only from outsiders; this was the pseudonym he was using in his negotiations for the Williamsburg Restoration in order not to turn the normal cupidity of landowners to avarice. He would have to supply the rest of the money himself, an undertaking that loomed larger every day that the Depression deepened. But when Raymond Fosdick asked him if it hadn't taken courage to assume obligations of this magnitude, he replied:

"I don't know whether it is courage or not. Often a man

gets into a situation where there is just one thing to do. There is no alternative. He wants to run, but there is no place to run to. So he goes ahead on the only course that's open, and people call it courage."

6

Clearing the Ground

With the project down to earth, and indeed "off the ground" in the sense of heading at last in a definite direction from which it would not swerve, the problems of clearing the land of 229 buildings and some 4,000 people presented themselves. Builders and developers know well the difficulties which this process can involve, although most people never have to encounter them and seldom hear about them. They are not aired in the press very much nor even in the courts to anything like the extent that the threats of legal action or publicity suggest.

Since most of the 299 ground leases in Columbia's Upper Estate had expired by the spring of 1930, and all but eighteen would lapse a year later, it might seem that there would be few obstacles in the way of razing the old brownstones. You might suppose that by the time the bulldozers and cranes and hoists and riveting machines were in full cry, the tenants of even the eighteen would be glad to go quietly.

New York real estate is not that simple. A great many of the houses, especially the comparatively new office and shop buildings on Fifth Avenue, were subleased, often to several subtenants. Few of them saw any good reason to give up a lease before they had to unless they were well paid. Most were willing to put up with a lot of noise and dirt all around until they got a price which can be regarded as anything from fair to exorbitant, depending upon which side of the bargaining you happened to favor.

A committee of three men with a staff of earnest aides worked on these negotiations from the spring of 1929 until late summer of 1931. In that time they bought up 250 leases and subleases for a total of more than $6 million—an average of just over $24,000 for each tenant who finally was persuaded to leave. When it came time to record with the County of New York the rights of the project to use the land on which it was to be built, 383 legal documents were filed to prove that all leases and subleases had been properly acquired. Of course that included the lots fronting on Sixth Avenue too.

One plot, however, remained unrecorded in this mass of paper. One massive brownstone remained inviolate, an impregnable castle defended fiercely along with its counterparts on either side. The struggle over Numbers 10, 12, and 14 West Forty-ninth Street enlivened the working days—and led to some sleepless nights—for a succession of Rockefeller aides for several years. Yet the leases on two of them had been among the first to expire in 1928 and Columbia had given prompt and due notice to the occupant that in accordance with the terms of their agreement, the university chose to purchase his buildings.

The recalcitrant tenant was William Nelson Cromwell, a

lawyer of imposing reputation and advanced age. He was seventy-six years old in 1930; his full, handsome face, mane of thick white hair, and heavy moustache gave him the appearance of an aging matinee idol made up for the role of a distinguished jurist. His firm, Sullivan & Cromwell, was one of the most eminent and expensive in the city—it still is—and he had been senior partner of it since 1887 when co-founder Algernon Sidney Sullivan died.

Cromwell had lived for many years at Number 12, held the lease on Number 14, and owned Number 10, which had been in the block that was sold to the Dutch Reformed Church and so no longer was part of the Upper Estate. He and his wife—they had no children—liked it where they were. The prospect of a few years of demolition and construction all around was less distasteful than uprooting their elderly bones from their old home and moving to strange new quarters. Also, it must be confessed, Cromwell had his belligerent moods, and he was understood by Columbia to be prepared to argue all the nice points of law and evidence which can be marshalled by a rich, determined, resourceful litigant. He intended to live and die at Number 12 West Forty-ninth Street, and he defied Columbia to put him out. As for Number 14, the controversy over that already was in arbitration and also dragged on for years.

It is as true in the arena of real estate law as anywhere else that it takes two to make a fight, and the university was not about to be one of them. Yet it was in a painful dilemma. The Rockefeller lease placed squarely upon the landlord the obligation to turn over the property as fast as leases expired. But strong hopes were entertained that Cromwell's will would contain a handsome bequest to his alma mater—he had taken his law degree there in 1876. After an eviction trial, win or lose, was he likely to be very generous? The stake might be very high, for Cromwell had been involved in many of the most important international and corporate cases of half a century, and his fees were reported to have run as high as $2 million for a single job.

Of course, he had a little more going for him than any implied blackmail, and indeed he himself never hinted at it. He could cite conversations with Columbia trustees which might be interpreted as giving him some vague oral rights to a renewal of his lease. On this basis, he was prepared to argue in court that he was justified in standing pat. He was understood by the University to be willing to commit the full resources of Sullivan & Cromwell to the fray, including the time and talent of all its eighty lawyers. The prospect of a confrontation with four score legal experts armed with zeal for the defense of their chief's hearth might well have dismayed more litigious groups than a board of university trustees. Columbia's board simply declined the gauge of battle.

Rockefeller was sympathetic. He himself had never enjoyed a lawsuit, and he had faith in the power of time and soft words to soothe the most fiery legal spirit. And he had time on his side, or so he thought. The south side of Forty-ninth Street near Fifth, where the Cromwell house stood, was not scheduled in building plans for several years at least, being in the area where, it was still hoped, the Metropolitan Opera might eventually find a new home. So Rockefeller was content to wait while one after another members of his staff took on the chore of persuading the stubborn Cromwell to move.

Their efforts dragged on for six years, and the exact combination of arguments and inducements which eventually led to an agreement is not quite clear. For one thing, the Rockefeller Center management thought that it could get along without Number 12 for as long as Cromwell was likely to live. For another, Cromwell was reported to have taken a fancy to the young head of the Rockefeller Center Renting

Department, Lawrence Kirkland, who also happened to be a lawyer. Kirkland's associates credited his Southern charm with an assist in inducing the eighty-two-year-old Cromwell to yield the most important point—most important to the Center although least important to him.

Actually, it was Dr. Butler of Columbia who brought the negotiations to a close. After a conversation between the two, Cromwell confessed he was deeply impressed by the improvements Rockefeller was bringing to the neighborhood and the city, and he decided he could do no less than follow the example. On February 20, 1936, he wrote a gracious letter to the university president referring to their talk and offering a settlement which was embodied in a formal agreement signed two months later.

It was a substantial victory for everybody concerned. With Rockefeller's consent, Columbia granted Cromwell possession of his home at Number 12 under a lease dated back to 1927 and running for a term of twenty-one years to January 31, 1948. In return, he terminated the arbitration proceedings concerning Number 14, taking a considerable loss. He also agreed that the building there could be demolished and a new one put up at any time.

The old gentleman outlived even this agreement, but when it expired in 1948 he was ninety-four years old and no one raised any question of eviction. He lingered on for months, finally dying in his own home, as he insisted he would, on July 19. Only after that did Rockefeller Center take over. Number 12 was purchased from Columbia and Number 10, from Cromwell's estate. They, along with Number 8, which Rockefeller had owned for a long time, were leased in a lump in 1949 to the Massachusetts Mutual Life Insurance Company to round out a plot acquired from the Dutch Reformed Church for a new office building.

Cromwell left one other legacy to the legend of Rockefeller Center. He had been a famous connoisseur of champagne, and no one was surprised that he should leave a considerable cellar. But demolition workmen who at last got into the old house at Number 12 were amazed—and momentarily delighted—to discover that his heirs had left a lot of it neatly racked in the old bins. The happy laborers seem to have been too excited to count as they began gathering in the lovely cool bottles. Later, after they opened some, they were too disappointed. Cromwell's wine had died even before he did; the champagne of a half dozen glorious vintages had turned to a thin, worthless vinegar.

Other lease holders fared better financially than Cromwell but probably did not have as much fun. One realty expert and his son, who had bought up thirteen Columbia ground leases over several years, sold them to the Center for $1,150,-000 in 1929. Two others nearly threw a legal monkey wrench into the machinery even more troublesome than Cromwell's although not so long drawn out. Part of the old lease agreements was that when Columbia announced it would exercise its right to take over the improvements, the price it would pay should be fixed by professional appraisers. In these two cases, the appraisal had not been completed by the time the lease actually expired, and the tenants argued that this automatically renewed the agreement for another twenty-one-year term. The lower court and first appeals court agreed with them. The state's highest court overruled the plea by a one-vote margin, and the lawyers could turn to some other legal and technical obstacles which stood in the way of their client's project.

First of all came the question of the Sixth Avenue properties, and while none provided the excitement of the Cromwell lease, they did pose problems. Indeed, one plot was completely unobtainable, the southeast corner of Sixth Avenue and Fiftieth Street, to the time this book was written a two-storied structure with a drug store on the street level. A Scotsman named John Maxwell owned it, and he would never consent to a price the Center considered reasonable. The northeast corner of Forty-ninth Street was bought all right, but an intransigent lessee was there, and so the biggest of the development's buildings has a little jog in the corner into which snuggles a well-known bar and tavern. In 1930 it was more discreetly labeled, but its business was the same and the operators, Daniel Hurley and Patrick Daly, had a lease which ran until 1942. Their asking price for that bit of paper was never met; they remained as tenants after it expired.

Another parcel, 70 West Fifty-first Street, belonged to a spinster of forbidding reputation, Miss Ella V. von E. Wendel. She was famous chiefly in real estate circles for carrying on the business principles of her father, whose rule for getting rich had been never to sell and never to improve a bit of land. At his death he owned a great deal of New York real estate on which others had built extensively. Miss Wendel finally agreed to lease her property for a term expiring with that of the Columbia agreement, and her estate sold it in 1935.

The next job for the lawyers was to determine what restrictions might hamper the development as planned. A generally restrictive covenant contained in all the deeds and leases forbade use of the property for any of the repulsive, noisome industries which had ruined many a handsome section of the city. Tanneries, soap boilers, glue factories, and such were prohibited, and one article of the Rockefeller lease preserves the ban well into the twenty-first century. The equally venerable covenants to maintain most of the lots for dwellings was another matter, and that was specifically dropped in a bundle of the usual documents in which everyone remotely concerned released everyone else from an outmoded obligation.

Columbia University's "Upper Estate" in 1930 just before demolition of the brownstone houses began. This photograph was taken from the corner of 51st Street and Sixth Avenue (now Avenue of the Americas) toward the southeast. In the left background are the spires of St. Patrick's Cathedral. The slender spire in the center is that of the Collegiate Church of St. Nicholas. The tracks in the near right corner were the Sixth Avenue Elevated Railroad.

Of course the actual physical clearing of the land began long before the paper work was completed. The wreckers moved in during the spring of 1930, first to the western end of the tract where the Radio City structures were to rise. But while the old brownstones crumbled and fell, the question of just what should replace them came in for some new soul searching.

The answer provided a strong international flavor which Rockefeller Center never lost. The idea of a cluster of buildings, each devoted to tenants of one foreign country, seems to have originated in the strivings to preserve some part of Rockefeller's earlier scheme to sublease land to tenants who would put up their own buildings. While it was not envisaged that the Center would escape responsibility for construction, it was hoped that the foreign countries, either officially or through semiofficial groups, would see to the renting of the space to their nationals.

Hugh S. Robertson, one of the senior partners of the Todd organization and destined to become executive manager of the Center, set the ball rolling with a trip to Europe in the summer of 1931. His early results were extremely encouraging. In October, agreements were signed with both English and French committees, and a British Empire Building and La Maison Francaise were the direct result. The British Building was destined to be the first to open in the Center except for the two theaters built for RKO. Located one on each side of the garden promenade which led from Fifth Avenue to the sunken plaza, it was inevitable that the British and French buildings should indirectly give their name to the strip, the "Channel Gardens."

Meanwhile, similar approaches were made to other countries. In due course there was talk of a Deutches Haus, a Pan-American Building, even a Russian Building. But the only one that came to anything was for a Palazzo d'Italia. And that did not materialize until the method of dealing with committees and governments, either officially or semiofficially, had collapsed.

It all went well enough through the ceremonial stages, cornerstone-laying with speeches by distinguished foreigners and dedications with music and banners. But the actual renting of shops and offices to solvent companies of the foreign country lagged until the committees were dissolved and the Center's own renting department took over that task. Then, indeed, enough tenants were found to give their true flavor—

and attract others so that the Palazzo d'Italia became just one wing of the International Building.

After that the principal intervention of outsiders in this phase of the development was an attempt by President Butler of Columbia, speaking for himself and a group of French scholars, to change the name of La Maison Francaise. They argued that this phrase lacked dignity, which they thought would be achieved with the title "La Maison de France." The discussion that followed was keen and erudite and no doubt contributed to the linguistic education of the participants. It is chiefly noteworthy today as an example of the sort of things that encumber the massive archives of modern enterprise.

A more important name problem arose with abandonment of the Metropolitan Square designation. While hope for the opera lingered on for years, the use of "Metropolitan" began to be considered inappropriate early in 1932. But what else to call it? In some newspaper accounts of the project it had been referred to as "Rockefeller City," but the public was beginning to use "Radio City" for the whole thing, not just the western section. John Todd argued for the name "Rockefeller" on the ground that it was a good drawing card.

"It's your money," Raymond Fosdick remembered him as saying during the course of one meeting. "Why not use the name?"

The biographer recalled that Rockefeller objected to having the family name "plastered on a real estate development." Nelson Rockefeller, who remembers his father's reluctance very well, adds that "we were only able to persuade him after considerable difficulty that this would be a sound thing and a creditable institution."

He yielded at last, and on April 27, 1932, the Metropolitan Square Corporation formally became Rockefeller Center, Inc. All that remained was to build it.

7
Of Steel, Stone, and Glass

In July, 1931, when excavators began drilling and blasting for the foundation sixty-eight feet down in Manhattan's bedrock, the Depression's greatest building project was already deeply committed. Thirteen companies by then were signed to contracts for the delivery of all the varied materials and fixtures that go into the making of a modern skyscraper—two hundred thousand tons of them for the RCA Building alone. Engineers and architects prepared schedules and plans for quantities and delivery dates so that each item would be on hand when it was needed, but not before—or so they hoped. Three of the city's leading building firms were also signed to cost-plus contracts for the actual construction.

The job gave employment to seventy-five thousand men on the spot and about twice as many working for suppliers and contractors elsewhere, so that at times it seemed that almost the only construction work in New York was at or for Rocke-feller Center. In virtually all the trades involved, it was a great thing to have any kind of a job in those days—few seg-ments of the economy were harder hit. The realization of this fact was as keen at the executive level as on the rough end of a shovel, so the work proceeded with a will and a harmony seldom equaled.

Wallace Harrison looks back on those first buildings as being without parallel in his experience for good teamwork and absence of crises or even difficulties. He also remembers as unique the advantage of being able to meet the unex-pected in a period of falling instead of rising prices; changes could be made and the new estimates would be lower than the old. It is almost axiomatic in the building world that any decision requiring a new supply of something means that the material, no matter what it is, will cost more than it would have last month and a great deal more than last year. But in the early construction of Rockefeller Center exactly the op-posite prevailed. It was estimated afterward that the total cost was about half what it would have been during the 1920's.

Men in the business today look back on the Depression prices as at a prehistoric era. In the RCA Building, for ex-ample, the erected steel cost $68 a ton; the limestone for the façade, from $1.83 to $1.48 a square foot; the window glass, 18 cents a square foot. Comparable prices in 1965 would be from five to ten times as much.

Cheapness never meant any sacrifice of quality, quite the contrary. In fact, his father's demand of quality is one of Nelson Rockefeller's chief impressions of this period. He had joined the enterprise shortly after his 1930 graduation from Dartmouth, first in the intricacies of the architectural and constructional offices and then on to renting. His father's in-sistence upon what he called "the last 5 percent" gave the early buildings an excellence in materials and workmanship which, in Nelson's opinion, is as much responsible for its success as its pioneering in design and scope. Rockefeller was everywhere with his four-foot rule and his questions—with his checkbook, too.

One day in 1932 he appeared at the weekly design meeting looking so drawn and limp that Harrison asked him if he was ill. The man whom all his subordinates were by now calling "Mr. Junior" shook his head.

"I couldn't sleep because I've been worrying how to finance all this," he explained. He added after a pause, "I've had to sell Standard Oil of New York at $2 a share." (It seemed only yesterday that the stock had been quoted at $80.)

It was one of his rare complaints about expense. And it did not keep him depressed for long. There were always absorbing details of design or engineering to ponder, some new problem on which to pass, some use for the four-foot rule. For he remained a fascinated observer of construction, and it is in this capacity that he made perhaps the greatest contribution of his career to the multitudes of his fellow citizens who shared his tastes. Not even Williamsburg nor the complete Rockefeller Center itself have done so much for so many whose only desire is to watch. Nelson has told the story with obvious relish.

"While work was at its busiest in the construction of the Center," he said, "my father stopped on the sidewalk to gaze down into a deep excavation where a big steam shovel was at work. You know how it is—the impulse that makes a crowd gather and watch men doing jobs with ponderous machines like a big steam shovel. Father has more than the average interest in that sort of thing, and he was standing there entranced, watching the jaws of the shovel close over a huge mouthful of rock and earth. A watchman employed on the job walked up to him and said in no uncertain tone: 'Move

along, buddy! You can't stand loafing here!' My father obedi-
ently moved along and didn't stand loafing there any more."

He did better. He struck a blow for loafers all over the
world by making them a welcome and almost official part of
every excavation job of any consequence anywhere. He ordered convenient windows cut in the solid wooden fences
around the site so people wouldn't have to look for a knot-
hole or a crack or crane their necks. Then followed proper
galleries to give spectators their rightful space.

"The best pilots stand on the shore." Some of them are at the
windows of this Sidewalk Superintendent's Club looking down
upon the excavation for the Eastern Air Lines Building in 1938.

Two far-reaching results have stemmed from this concession to that normal human impulse to watch machinery at
work. First, the idea was so widely copied and so acclaimed
that few people today would dare try to dig a big hole out of
sight of the public because he'd probably be suspected of
some dark, nefarious plot. Builders even provide music and
baseball scores and pretty pictures to go with the convenient
windows. Secondly, the public relations department of
Rockefeller Center hit upon organization of a Sidewalk
Superintendents Club to lend further prestige to idleness.
Membership cards were printed up with a seal and handed

out on request. Chapters were formed in other cities. There was even a national convention of them in 1939. It was no small thing to have conferred upon millions of urban loafers the respectable status of Sidewalk Superintendent, secure in the window provided by no longer arrogant builders and in the club's motto, *"De beste stuurlui staan aan wal,"* an old Dutch proverb that means "the best pilots stand on the shore."

The motto might well have served as Rockefeller's own throughout his general direction of the Center. He stood on the shore, observing the trials and tribulations of his managers, advisers, and assorted assistants, and guided them wisely even when the shoals seemed uncomfortably close. Many of the decisions were routine enough, but they all were needed to advance the work, and in the long run no one but he could make them.

So seemingly simple a question as linking the various buildings by underground passageways, with shops and restaurants serving the pedestrian, called for a vast amount of negotiation. An arrangement was made with the city and state while architects and engineers and builders grappled with the physical problems. The passageways, to be of any real use, would have to burrow under city streets, and the law provided that while one city administration could give the permit, another could take it away. The prospect of having very expensive installations subject to the whim of New York's Board of Estimate after every election was hardly attractive. The State Legislature was prevailed upon to enact a new law authorizing the city to give Rockefeller Center a twenty-five-year permit for rights under Forty-ninth and Fiftieth streets, revocable earlier than that only on a showing of a positive overriding public need. After that, various authorizations permitted the underground maze to be built with reasonable assurances of permanence.

The logistics of construction is about as complicated as that of an army in the field, and a flaw in the lines of supply can be as disastrous to the building as to troops. When you are using cement by the thousands of barrels, cinders and sand by the hundreds of truckloads, reinforcing rods by the mile, and bricks by the million, you have to be sure they arrive in order as needed, and that a few of the many thousands of tons of steel do not come along ahead of them—or too far behind. The stuff is shipped from dozens of different firms in almost as many industries. Someone once listed the major items that went into a single Rockefeller Center building. There were sixty, ranging from aluminum spandrels and sills to tile roofing. The unsung heroes of this business are the men who work at desks and telephones to maintain a semblance of reason in the logistics.

If the slide into depression kept prices of material down, it did even worse for rents. During the first couple of years of excavating and building, the economic position of the country generally worsened steadily. As the Center began to take shape—the two big theaters, the RCA Building steel rising into the clouds, the massive thirty-one-story RKO Building, the six-story British and French buildings on either side of the Channel Gardens—it was freely predicted that none of them could ever possibly attract enough solvent tenants to break even.

In the summer of 1932, the nadir of the Depression in many ways, these prophecies seemed to be coming true even before a tenant could move in. The first two structures scheduled for completion were the RKO theaters, both planned for spectacular openings before the end of the year. But while broadcasting was proving depression-proof, motion pictures were much more vulnerable, and RKO was in serious difficulties, complicated by the government's antitrust suit to split the whole RCA complex from its parent com-

Steelworkers walk across a newly-placed beam of the RCA Building in 1932.

panies. And RCA not only owed these parents money, it had not as yet showed a profit, so it would have to think of retrenchments.

Actually, it was clear, RCA was not going to need much more than half the million square feet of office space for which it had contracted. The National Broadcasting Company either could not or did not want to pay the $500,000 it was supposed to contribute to the cost of its studios. RKO was heading shakily toward a receivership even as some of its offices, the very first to be ready for occupancy in October, were opened for business.

When the dust of controversy and confusion settled, the whole structure of the industry had been changed. RCA was on its own under the general direction of David Sarnoff, and Rockefeller Center was ruefully reducing its estimate of renting income. Under a revised agreement, RCA was to pay during its first year only about one eighth of the sum originally expected, and not until the fifth year would it be as much as half. A note payable in five years without interest was accepted in lieu of NBC's cash contribution. RCA did give up some special privilege clauses in its original lease and turned over stock which the Center eventually sold for the equivalent of about two years of the original rent.

That momentarily settled the difficulties with RCA, but not those involving the theaters. The two opened as planned in December, but within a month RKO was bankrupt, and the leases on the two houses, the Radio City Music Hall and the New Roxy, soon to be renamed the Center Theater, automatically terminated. Claims for damages as a result of this liquidation went in and out of court for the next seven years before a complicated settlement was finally reached in 1939. Meantime, the two theaters were placed temporarily in the hands of two RKO subsidiaries which were not in receivership.

It was all one more lesson for the Rockefeller Center management that there is seldom any good substitute for doing the distasteful chore yourself. The great enterprise had been conceived as a mere leasing arrangement—the Rockefeller management would have no concern with construction, no maintenance, and no worries about rents and vacancies and keeping tenants happy. Now it was deep in the biggest private building project ever attempted, scurrying the world over in search of individual tenants for shops and offices, reconciling itself to building up an army of employees to take care of all these people and finally, as the country waited for newly elected President Franklin D. Roosevelt to take office in March, getting ready to run the city's two newest theaters. One might be forgiven for feeling that if this was the fruit of so much careful planning to place responsibility on others, the fatalists who said you could not ever escape your future had something.

8

The Curtain Rises

That future had been mercifully obscured, certainly so far as the theaters were concerned, when the morning papers of December 27, 1932, carried modest advertisements—modest in size, that is—for "The Greatest Show in the World in the World's Greatest Theater." Appropriately enough, in view of the public interest, the first completed segment of the project which, three years earlier, had been conceived as providing a new home for fashionable entertainment was now opening with a more plebian show but in a setting quite as splendid as the opera would have attempted. Ominously, the opening was in an economic climate that would ensure deficits rivaling those of opera for a long time.

The Radio City Music Hall lived up to the advertised boast of "world's greatest theater" in size and, in the eyes of a very large number of people, in decor and comfort and the-

Radio City Music Hall—the proscenium arch is 60 feet high and the stage a city block wide. The Rockettes are on stage, the Radio City Music Hall Symphony Orchestra in the pit.

atrical efficiency. It held 6,200 seats; its lobbies and corridors were as spacious as those of any opera house; it had the largest stage in the world, 144 feet by 67, with a 43-foot revolving stage in the middle and hydraulic pistons that could raise and lower any one of three sections on the whole stage itself. The proscenium arch was breathtaking; the golden curtain weighed three tons. The backstage facilities, the organ, and a rising and descending platform for a whole symphony orchestra were fabulous. It could measure its lovely rich curtains, drapes, and specially woven carpeting by the acre. Paintings and statuary by distinguished artists—not of the most modern style, to be sure—abounded in lobbies, corridors, and men's and women's lounges.

The Music Hall was the creation of one of New York's most ebullient showmen, so far as any individual can be credited with such a work. Roxy—only his family and a few close friends and associates knew or cared that he had a more conventional name, Samuel Lionel Rothafel—had operated by far the most widely acclaimed motion picture theater in New York, which bore his own nickname, and he was the acknowledged genius of his trade. RKO was generally considered to have brought off an admirable coup when they persuaded him to take over the management of the new Music Hall.

Even before it opened, it had made a great impression on people. An incident which gives a clue to why, and also to Roxy's thinking, occurred during a European study trip which a group of Rockefeller Center's best minds undertook in the summer of 1931. Roxy, along with Wallace Harrison, Reinhard, Chief Engineer O.B. Hanson of NBC, and Peter Clark, the greatest stage builder of his day, looked over the latest the Continent offered in theaters. They were rewarded with some useful ideas, especially in the new Moscow houses built between 1919 and 1922 by a group of brilliant young Russian architects who disappeared on Stalin's rise to power. But Roxy's real inspiration came from a far larger scene than any Europe had to offer. Standing on the deck of their ship in mid-Atlantic at sunset one day on the return trip, the passengers were treated to a magnificent spectacle.

"That's what I want for the Music Hall!" Roxy exclaimed, and as nearly as builders and decorators could do it, that is just about what he got.

Roxy also ended a terrible hassle over the color scheme for the auditorium. After about ten different combinations had been presented and rejected, he begged: "Would you please give me gold for the ceiling and red for the chairs. That's my good luck sign."

Physically, the result was a triumph for Rockefeller Center as a whole. Not the least of its effect was the almost awesome contrast it offered to the economy of the country at that very unfestive season of the Depression's worst year. Sharing the news of the opening was a proposal, seriously propounded by a group of scientific leaders, to give up money as we had become accustomed to it and substitute an electric or, as some put it, an Edison dollar. It was to be equal to 40 kilowatt hours, and its sponsors thought it would perhaps end the Depression.

(The electrical industry, however, was not enjoying peak popularity just then. Also sharing the front page this day was an announcement that the Greek government refused to extradite Samuel Insull, perhaps the chief American villain of the moment; he had pyramided a dizzying collection of electric utility companies into one of the most expensive financial houses of cards ever put together. When it collapsed, thousands of families lost their savings and millions clamored for justice against what few denied had been a gigantic fraud.)

In the public mood engendered by such reading matter, and by the foreshadowing of a money crisis which would reach its climax in the closing of all the banks in the country within a few weeks, the ambitious entertainment which Roxy had assembled for this Tuesday night fell short of the billing he gave it. His purpose was to revive in classic two-a-day form the old supremacy of vaudeville, virtually killed in the United States by the movies and radio—and maybe a little by changing public taste. But he proposed to establish it on a far grander scale than it had known in its heyday. He was nothing if not extravagant. So for this occasion he engaged enough talent to have launched three or four theaters.

For his master of ceremonies, Roxy reached back to the gilded days of the Weber & Fields Broadway Music Hall, which graced the top of the circuit at the turn of the century. He came up with a singing comedian who was a star then and had a big following still. This was DeWolf Hopper, a name to conjure with in the theater ever since he had made "Casey at the Bat" famous. But he was seventy-four years old now and showed his fifty-three years on the stage.

Hopper presided over a staggering list of singing, dancing, acrobatic, and comic acts, and some of them were rather loftier in tone and execution than the old vaudeville patrons had been exposed to, except occasionally one at a time and briefly, with advance billing that this was a very special item. Besides all the usual top acts of the profession, and about twice as many as usual, there appeared a leading singer from the Berlin Opera, a Metropolitan basso, the Tuskegee Choir, Martha Graham and her dancers, and a Kreutzberg ballet. Leon Leonidoff was production director (thereafter senior producer at the Music Hall), and it is one of the marks of his genius that people do not always remember it.

The house was full by only a little after the scheduled curtain time of eight o'clock. Of course, it was also filled with holders of free passes to a degree which probably no one ever tried to learn. The announced prices were 99 cents to $2.50, and some of the audience were reminded of the old Hippodrome a little further down Sixth Avenue where circuses and a variety of spectacular shows had attracted enormous audiences before World War I. But, these reminiscent ones hastened to add, it was a Hippodrome with all the best modern improvements.

Newspapers carried long stories about the opening on their front pages, with feature comment and pictures inside, and the pictures were impressive. The words were not so pleasing to the theater's management. Brooks Atkinson in *The New York Times* was bluntly unenthusiastic and, unfortunately, thoroughly representative of his critical brethren. The best he could say about the show itself was that it had been "more the product of a radio and motion picture mind than of a genius for the short turns and encores of the music hall stage." One doubts that Atkinson would have been quite so gentle if he had seen the whole performance. He obviously did not, because he got his review written in time for Wednesday morning's paper.

Another member of that first night audience has the best of reasons for remembering it. He is G. S. Eyssell, who has come to the presidency of Rockefeller Center by way of the Radio City Music Hall's management, although at the time he had no connection with either. A theater man from Kansas City, Missouri, who had been transferred to New York after successful movie house operations in California and Texas, he was with Paramount at the end of 1932. This company, too, had grandiose theater ideas; their New York house on Times Square was the city's leader when it was built into the firm's massive office building five years before. As a guest at the Music Hall's first night, Eyssell manages to be polite. Asked how he liked the performance, he replied mildly: "The performance was quite long."

Actually, it lasted for hours past the normal time for a New York final curtain, and as Eyssell warms to his recollection, he becomes more explicit: "The audience started to leave about one o'clock," he says, "and I think they had finished filing out by two—at least it seemed that late to me. The house had emptied, but the show was still going on . . . Yes, I myself stayed to the bitter end."

Before the town had a chance to catch its breath, Rockefeller Center's second opening of the week was upon it, and this time Roxy was in his own element. In the block below the Music Hall had been erected what he called "my intimate theater." It had 3,700 seats, 2,500 fewer than its sister up the street. But it had been planned for the sort of entertainment at which its impresario had made his reputation, a picture palace showing a first class film plus a stage show. Furthermore, it was named in his honor the RKO Roxy. (The plain Roxy, owned by Fox, refused to relinquish the title just because it had lost the man.) For the first picture he had obtained "The Animal Kingdom," an adaptation of a very popular Philip Barry play.

Although this opening was only two days after that of the Music Hall, it had a rather more gala atmosphere because of the unusually large swarm of celebrities who attended. Many of them were screen personalities who had not been specially interested in a two-a-day house. They, in turn, attracted such a crowd of street watchers that the police had to call for reserves to help control the autograph seekers and just plain pushers. Inside, the performance was well received, and *The New York Times* graciously acknowledged that "Roxy gave New York a thrill" with his second new house.

A month to the day from the Music Hall's premiere, RKO was in receivership, setting in train all the complexities of a change in management. But already some such change had been seen to be not only in the cards but in the works. Within two weeks, the RKO management realized that two-a-day vaudeville, at least the Roxy version of it, was not going to keep all that magnificence going. The first sixteen days of it lost a cool $180,000, and in 1933 that amount of money was a lot cooler than before or after. On January 11, RKO decided to switch the big theater's program to a film plus stage show and restrict the RKO Roxy to film alone. In so doing, it gave Rockefeller Center a future president.

The president of RKO, Harold B. Franklin, had talked to Eyssell reservedly about the Music Hall's problems only a few days after the debut; the two men had known and worked with each other when they represented their respective firms in California. A few days later, he invited Eyssell to work out of his office at RKO as a troubleshooter, and the first trouble to be shot was finding pictures for the Music Hall.

"It had no pictures at the time, of course," he recalls, "and they were mighty few and far between, especially the good ones. But we were fortunate in being able to grab for our opening film a Columbia attraction, 'The Bitter Tea of General Yen.' Then it turned out we had no sound equipment for such pictures, and it all had to be rushed in and installed in a few days."

What with shifting policies, RKO's bankruptcy, and a serious illness which incapacitated Roxy from right after the opening until the following May, the management had its hands full. This soon became a committee of six on which Rockefeller Center and RCA had equal representation. Eyssell remembers not only the scramble for pictures—the Music Hall had to change nearly every week its first year—but scurrying about to sell groups of New Yorkers on the idea of coming to the show. This was not easy, in spite of a 35-cent admission charge before noon and 55 cents in the afternoon. In normal times, such places can count upon crowds of out-of-towners; often they are the mainstay of the business. But in 1933 hardly any visitors came to New York and most of those who did could not afford to take in shows. However, "The Bitter Tea of General Yen," now a film classic greeted with such expressions as "archaic but interesting" by *The New York Times* when it was revived, took in $81,083 at the box office for an eight day run.

The Roosevelt New Deal started that spring, and there was some feeling in the air that maybe the Depression would not last forever. But such traces of optimism were not reflected at the box office. During the bank holiday in March, admissions were sold for scrip, for postdated checks, and for IOU's—"anything," says Eyssell, "to get the people in." Only eight of the forty-seven pictures shown in 1933 topped or reached the gross take of the first.

A scene from the pageant of "The Nativity," a traditional part of every Christmas show at the Music Hall.

It was not much easier when the committee form of management gave way to the Radio City Music Hall Corporation, a joint enterprise of Rockefeller Center and RCA at first, but soon acquired entirely by the Center. One of its members on the old committee, W. G. Van Schmus, became president with Eyssell as secretary. Shortly before this, in January 1934, Roxy, who had never fully recovered his health, resigned. The new corporation had already lost any right it might have retained to use his name. The highest New York State court had ruled the previous May that it belonged to the old Roxy, and the United States Supreme Court refused to review that decision. So the "intimate" theater became the Center Theater in July.

The Music Hall, competing desperately for popular movies without outstanding success, was making an unrivaled name for its stage shows. Senior Producer Leonidoff proved a master at arranging spectacles which took full advantage of the huge stage and uncanny mechanical facilities. In the winter of 1933 and spring of 1934, he started what has become a tradition of splendid Christmas and Easter shows which seem to pack the place no matter what the accompanying picture may be.

The associate producer, Russell Markert, trained the precision dancers who became almost better known than their home. Markert had pioneered this sort of thing with sixteen girls on the stage of the old Missouri Theater in St. Louis in 1925. He called them "The Rockets" and brought them to New York for a Broadway run. They never went back. Roxy engaged them for his own theater, had Markert enlarge the troupe, and changed the name to "Roxyettes." They had been one of the numbers on that interminable December 27 bill and became a feature of the short-lived stage show at the Center Theater. They came over to the Music Hall when the new policy was adopted, and after Roxy's departure, their name was changed to "Rockettes." These talented young women not only gave new meaning to this particular form of the dance, but they had a good deal to do with revolutionizing the American concept of "chorus girl."

The solid reputation of the stage shows was an investment, but at the time no one could be sure it would pay off. They were based and nurtured, says Eyssell today, on the one word that Rockefeller insisted upon as a key to the whole center: "quality." In spite of the balance sheet, no one was allowed to skimp on a Music Hall stage presentation. Eyssell recalls that one reason the theaters were not leased to any of the major film companies after RKO's failure was his own argument that, good as these firms might be, they would not maintain the standards which Rockefeller Center demanded.

"For that matter," he adds, "the companies took a very cautious look at us, and an appraisal. They were not so sure by any means that the Music Hall was going to be a success. After all, all we had then were a lot of expenses and very little income."

The Center Theater was proportionately as long on expenses and had even less income. There was no hope of getting enough first-run pictures for two theaters, even if it had been sound to run them in competition with each other. So the Center Theater, as elegant in its way as the Music Hall, was reduced to second- and sometimes third-run movies, although it never was quite so desperate as to try double features as many of New York's elegant old legitimate theaters did. Even at a minimum admission charge of 25 cents and with the bill changed twice a week, it was seldom filled.

After suffering through a protracted period of public apathy, it was closed for a time, and then in 1935 a new agency was organized to operate it by leasing it for live shows. It was in great demand for a variety of entertainments which would have had to be subsidized—a second-string Metropolitan Opera Company, a repertory theater to be headed by Eva LeGalliene, a lyric theater, and a French revue-cum-restaurant are remembered. But after its experiences so far, the Center Theater's management easily resisted the temptation to become financially embroiled.

The trouble was that while the place might be intimate by Roxy's standards, it was much too big for the average play and even for most musicals. But it was admirably suited to extravaganzas, to spectacles, and to operatic performances. Some success, even of a monetary nature, was won with a few productions—"The Great Waltz" and "White Horse Inn" were perhaps the most memorable—and then ice shows were popular for ten years. In between editions of the ice shows, the Center Theater was kept open by the appearances of the San Carlo Opera Company, so at last Rockefeller Center was the home, if only for twelve days at a time, of the musical art form which brought it into being.

Without a very long purse behind them, it is plain that neither of these houses could have survived the Depression.

As it was, the Music Hall went for three years before it began to make a profit. However, it dared hold a picture for more than seven days quite early, although the management was apprehensive. In April 1933, it ran "Cavalcade," a nostalgic Noel Coward rhapsody on the glory of England, for two solid weeks. People came for the second just as gratifyingly as for the first. "Little Women" ran three weeks the same year. Later on, the management was much less worried than it had been for these two when it kept Disney's "Snow White" for a dazzling five weeks.

Now all this time, the rest of Rockefeller Center was going up, offstage, so to speak. By the time the Music Hall was in the black in 1935, the two major blocks of the whole development, all the area between Forty-ninth and Fifty-first streets from Fifth to Sixth avenues, had been completely built except for a site fronting on Rockefeller Plaza and running west to the eastern wall of the Music Hall. Not, however, without a certain amount of pain and potshots mingled with the pleasure and praise.

9

Brickbats and Bouquets

It was too bad that John D. Rockefeller, Jr., had acquired the habit of not reading newspapers when bad news was in the offing. If he had been familiar with the stern disapproval of *The New York Times'* editorial page on the showing of the first Rockefeller Center model in March, 1931, the memory would have added to his pleasure in a letter early in December, 1933, from John H. Finley, the presiding genius of that page. Dr. Finley wrote:

I wish that you could have seen your high tower as I saw it from a *Times* window in the late afternoon light on Thanksgiving Day—a shaft of rose color rising from the gray buildings in the foreground. I have since found this line which describes it better than any words of mine: 'a rose red city half as old as time.' It turned to a deeper color as the light changed and it was ever more impressive. I am now quite reconciled and grateful.

On the other hand, perhaps it was just as well that he did not read his press clippings as avidly as some other men, for he would have been greeted with this from Lewis Mumford in *The New Yorker* that same month:

The mice have labored, and they have brought forth their mountain. Like most of the things that were conceived during the last days of the boom, the central building is very big. And when one has said this, one has said almost everything. Shall we leave it at that—or shall we dwell on the holes and the little scratchy toothmarks the mice have left in their cheese?

Mumford chose to dwell for three of *The New Yorker* columns. He thought the center looked well under artificial lighting at night because "one can forget that every touch of ornament is bad with an almost juvenile badness." The thin slab of the RCA Building "looks like the scrawniest of towers." He condemned the Channel, the lower plaza, the art, and the interiors and concluded:

Architecturally, in short, Rockefeller Center is much ado about nothing. It lacks the distinction, the strength, the confidence of good architecture just because it lacks any solidness of purpose and sincerity of intention. On the one hand, the projectors have eaten into a colossal fortune with a series of bad guesses, blind stabs, and grandiose inanities; on the other, they have trimmed and played for a decent mediocrity. And the whole effect of the Center is mediocrity—seen through a magnifying glass."

No wonder a friend, advising Colonel Wood of this article, added, "I suggest you have about three good cocktails before reading. You will need three after reading."

Walter Lippmann, the country's leading journalistic pundit in the field of government but fortunately not regarded as quite so omniscient in the arts, already had complained that "the esthetic aimlessness of the enterprise is equaled only by its social irresponsibility." And, referring to

A Rockefeller Center guide points to the view to the south—dominated by the Empire State Building—from the Observation Roof of the RCA Building. Mr. Junior's little Gothic fence is only partly obscured by the visitors.

the Music Hall, which he called "a pedestal to sustain a peanut," he concluded: "What use could be made of it, what esthetic, what human, what social purposes the contraption would serve are questions apparently reserved for the cold, gray dawn of the morning after."

Most New York citizens were not as sensitive as either Mumford or Lippmann. They were much more impressed by the magnitude of the Center as it was developing and even basked a bit in civic pride. Once more Gotham was able to boast of the biggest and the best of its kind.

The tower to which Finley and Mumford referred con-

tained the one architectural feature that was included solely
to please the man for whom the development was named.
Rockefeller wanted a little fence of pure Gothic design
around the topmost roof of the RCA Building. Harrison,
telling about it indulgently, gives the impression that the
architects humored him, although it had no relevance to anything else, because they supposed no one could see it. Mr.
Junior, however, was farsighted—literally—and Harrison used
to see him on the street gazing up at his railing with ap-
proval. It has since become almost a Rockefeller trademark.
Every photograph taken from this vantage point, one of the
favorites for shooting a New York panorama, includes a bit of
this distinctive Gothic in the foreground.

The building itself had been completed on May 1, 1933,
sixteen months after construction began. The British Empire
Building had opened a month earlier; La Maison Francaise
followed in August, and the International Buildings completed the two blocks of the center in April, 1935. The problems now were to get tenants and to line up prospects for the
structures that would be erected on the other side of Forty-
ninth Street.

In seeking its solutions, Rockefeller Center had been pursuing a double barreled approach for two years. One was a
conventional renting department headed by the young Kirkland, who was to persuade Lawyer Cromwell to be reasonable. The other was operated in a sort of lone ranger fashion by
Nelson A. Rockefeller, Mr. Junior's second son, twenty-two
years old at the time he began.

Young Rockefeller had spent the year after his graduation
from Dartmouth on a wedding trip around the world. Immediately after his return in 1931, Rockefeller Center, to
whose board of directors he had been elected during his
senior year in college, became one of his introductions to the
business world. It was only one because for a time he spent

his mornings at the Chase National Bank, of which his uncle, Winthrop Aldrich, was president. Nelson much preferred selling leases to banking, and his connection with Chase was brief.

In New York, mere desire does not make a real estate broker, even when coupled with talents and connections; a license is required. Nelson studied briefly but intensively, passed the necessary examination, and then went out every afternoon—after he left Chase, every morning, too—calling on prospects. He was young and inexperienced but, as he now points out with a smile, he was the lucky possessor of a name that opens doors.

"I was able to get in to talk to people who wouldn't have seen most men my age," he says.

It was not just his name, however, that got the interviewees to sign leases. He also had to offer an attractive proposition, and he worked out a plan of action which brought a steady trickle of tenants to the new buildings. It also earned him a good income in commissions, for he was an independent operator, not employed by his father or his father's company.

"I found that many companies were looking for new quarters in spite of the Depression," he explains. "Either their old offices were too cramped or too old-fashioned or in a wrong location. I was able to give them certain concessions, mostly taking over the lease on their old space for the rest of their lease. Then I'd look around for somebody to rent that."

He set up his own short-lived corporation for this operation, which earned commissions on the Rockefeller Center space he rented and on the subleases of the old space. He proved so successful at it that the venerable August Heckscher, owner of the Heckscher Building a few blocks up Fifth Avenue and an eminent figure in the city's business and philanthropy for at least as long as Nelson's grandfather, sued him—and Rockefeller Center and his father and everybody else involved—for $10 million. Heckscher charged that his tenants had been lured away unfairly or by coercion. In the heat of legal combat, his spokesman denounced this "modern Frankenstein," although whether they meant to compare the Rockefellers to Mary Shelley's fictional student or the buildings to the monster he created was not clear. Neither Heckscher nor his estate ever pushed the case to trial and, finally, it was dropped.

Other real estate men continued to protest the Rockefeller tactics. They said cut rates for the first part of a lease's term and the taking over of space in other buildings was unethical. However, it seems that the critics were all men who lost desirable tenants or clients; both practices were quite common at the time, as every landlord struggled to keep the people he had and replace those he had lost.

Old-timers remember that the chief effect of the Heckscher suit on Rockefeller Center was apprehension lest one of the new companies just about to be landed for a big block of offices, American Cyanamid, back out. They were planning to move from another Fifth Avenue structure, the Ruppert Building, while Nelson took over their old quarters. This building was owned by Colonel Jacob Ruppert, owner of a well-known beer company and a baseball team, the Yankees. If he, too, became unpleasant or litigious, it could be serious. But the colonel was pleased. He said he preferred to have a lot of small businesses to having one big one, and there was no doubt he would keep the tenants who subleased American Cyanamid's quarters.

Opinions of Rockefeller Center improved over the years, both as to its artistic and its commercial merits. On the last point, eventually profitable operations in big figures constitute an irrefutable argument. But beauty remains in the eye of the beholder. Within a decade of the Mumford-Lippmann fulminations, the critical eyes that looked at Rockefeller Center belonged to a new generation and saw an entirely different place. Some of the comments strike one as equally extreme, however. The Center's most avid admirer among architects is Winston Weisman, who has written about it in professional journals more than once. To him it is "important not only as art and architecture, but as a social and historical document as well." He added: "It is to this country what the Pyramids of Gizeh were to Egypt, the Baths of Caracalla to Imperial Rome, the Cathedral of Rheims to Gothic France."

A more restrained architectural comment is that Rockefeller Plaza, probably responsible for more refashioning of more real estate than any other feature of Rockefeller Center, is "the quintessence of city planning." Jane Jacobs, an eminent city planning expert, thinks the "extra street" concept of the plaza is the reason the whole project has become such "a center of use." Harrison sums up what is perhaps the most important claim:

It was the first time a group of skyscrapers ever was planned as a group. If Rockefeller Center had not been built, there would be no basis to say how other groups could be done, as they have been done, mostly with government money, in a number of cities since.

The thinking that produced Rockefeller Center, that the buildings are for the people who use them, has gone into all our architecture now. We see a wonderful example right next door to us in the last building Eero Saarinen built. [We were talking as this new home for the Columbia Broadcasting System neared completion in 1965.] That is a return to the fundamental principle we established in 1930 as to what good office space was in New York City—a solid pier and a window, a pier and a window. There has never been anything as flexible and CBS has come back to it.

This perhaps interested opinion was succinctly confirmed by a Swiss art historian, Siegfried Giedion, who remarked:

"Rockefeller Center simply is in advance of its period in the urban scale. What must change is not the Center but New York itself."

Finally, Edward Durell Stone replied when asked in 1964 what he thought was the best example of an owner who aspired to achieve a great building:

I would say Rockefeller Center, which I still find the exemplar of private enterprise, when it comes to architecture. I remember that one of the New York newspapers ridiculed Mr. Rockefeller as a wild-eyed visionary, squandering the old man's money . . . Well, Mr. Rockefeller was a visionary. That's the thing you need to get great architecture. He employed the best talent of the time, and built well.

A layman trying to account for the difference between critics writing about Rockefeller Center in its infancy and those of its maturity can find a couple of explanations. For one thing, the second group have had the advantage of hindsight, of appraising the finished job. But also they are reconciled to the idea that this big chunk of midtown real estate had to be developed, in view of modern conditions, as a complex of skyscrapers. In the carping of the early objectors one detects a wistful yearning for the low, pleasing lines of the urban architecture of the long gone past. Why, they seem to ask querulously, shouldn't Rockefeller Center have captured the grace of the Renaissance in Florence, the lawns and palaces of Westminster, the spaciousness of Haussmann's Paris? With eyes focussed on the horizontal, they were incapable of throwing back their heads to see what an entire group of tall buildings might look like against the sky.

The good things and the bad said about the new development did have one effect in common. They brought it to the attention of the public. The apocryphal saying attributed to a number of politicians, "I don't care what you say about me,

but be sure you spell my name right," has some validity for a
real estate operation. It helps if yours is a household word.
Even if the esthetics are damned and the purpose deplored,
many businesses find it advantageous to take offices or shops
in a location so well known. And Rockefeller Center was
becoming very well known indeed. In the year the RCA
Building opened, *The New York Times* carried no fewer
than 130 news stories about the Center, not all of them un-
favorable.

What with such publicity added to normal renting practices and the Nelson Rockefeller salesmanship, the vast spaces
of the Center, by far the biggest commercial office complex
ever completed, gradually filled up. The record of solvency
among the tenants was high, too. A special drive for oil companies, which in a motorized country are nearly as depression-
proof as broadcasting, brought in a considerable roster,
headed understandably by Standard Oil. A good many of the
firms which had supplied materials or services for the construction were induced to make the Center their New York
headquarters, and some of them stayed after the work was
finished.

What some regard as a pardonable blunder was committed
when the precedent of NBC's privilege in the RCA lease
giving NBC a monopoly of broadcasting was followed in a
variety of other fields. Exclusive rights were granted for the
only barber shop, news gathering agency (Associated Press),
cutlery store, rubber company, language school, and bank.

For example, the Chase Bank was conceded the sole banking privileges in a lease under which the institution eventually opened three branches in three different Center buildings. Not until 1940 was this corrected. By then it was clear
that Rockefeller Center had become in virtually every sense,
except that of having a place to sleep, a "city within a city."
It could not afford to give a banking monopoly, not even to

one with a close family relationship. Tenants wanted their own banks handy, so after eight years Chase was induced to relinquish its exclusive contract. As a result, fourteen banking institutions were eventually established in the Center. Gradually, almost all the other exclusive privileges were withdrawn.

Other favorites for leasing then—and now, for that matter —were transportation and travel companies and foreign consulates or information offices. They have multiplied in what must be an exceptionally suitable environment: 112 of them were there when this book was written. A further international flavor was provided by New York branches of foreign companies. All these gave a nice tone to Rockefeller Center, and were good, solid, rent-paying tenants, too.

Then, for they had been planned when the site was to be a home for the opera, the myriad shops above and below ground were a matter of anxious consideration. The primary aim was a group that would attract a lot of people and make a lot of money. But in buildings of the prestige Rockefeller Center was seeking this must be qualified. The people attracted must not grossly offend the office tenants and visitors; the money must be made in a dignified manner without excessive fanfare and from the sale of goods that befit the surroundings. One commodity was ruled out from the beginning. Although by 1933 thirteen years of national Prohibition was obviously doomed—the extremely temperate Rockefeller had come out against it, and repeal was one of the pledges of the victorious Roosevelt—it was ruled in deference to the family's temperance that no liquor would be sold by the bottle but served only in the restaurants and clubs.

On the whole, Rockefeller Center was successful in achieving its shop objectives. But the mortality of such establishments in the 1930's was high. Most of the leases called for 10 percent of the gross revenue as rent and, in any case, a certain minimum. Many of the early tenants could not make the minimum, but a departure for purely financial reasons was largely a phenomenon of the prewar years. After that, the shop tenants shook down pretty well to the sort who could prosper in these surroundings.

Not the least of the difficulties concerned the underground maze of corridors and concourse which connected all the buildings in a subterranean version of the second-story promenade which had once been conceived as a rival to the *Place de l'Opera*. Eventually, there was more than a mile of it. Besides being a convenient way to get from one Rockefeller Center structure to another in bad weather, the concourse was planned to link up with the station of a new Sixth Avenue subway. But the rackety old elevated train still ran. In due time the subway was built, and with something more than fifteen million passengers using the station every year, the concourse finally got the pedestrian traffic for which it was designed.

It made the ordinary New York subway station look like a poor relation. In order to soften the contrast, the Center acquired rights to the station's mezzanine from the city's Transit Authority and remade it in keeping with the Center's ideas of lighting, decoration, and (which was widely commented upon as a contrast to nearly all the rest of the subway system) cleanliness. The demonstration that stations do not have to be dingy had some beneficial effect in other parts of the system, although riders may think not enough.

While the old elevated tracks still stood, the Rockefeller Center renting burden was increased by the search for tenants to fill up buildings not yet built, nor even fully designed. The needs of a major tenant, one who would contract for enough space to warrant calling the building by his name, would have to be taken into account in the layout, and even in the external shape. With the completion of the International Building in 1935, there remained all the Columbia land on the south side of Forty-ninth Street except for the Center Theater and a big empty space between the Plaza and the Music Hall.

The latter was disposed of by a lease to The Associated Press, largest of American news services; the peculiar demands of the tenant dictated the comparatively blocky, fifteen-story silhouette of the structure bearing its name at 50 Rockefeller Plaza and 34 West Fifty-first Street. The architects wrestled manfully to reconcile their over-all concept of the Center with the AP's demand for several floors with so much space on each that the building would have to rise sheer from the outermost building line all around. The way the dilemma of design was finally avoided was, as Harrison recalls: "Harry Hofmeister went over in a corner, spoke to no one, and got the building done."

On the other side of Forty-ninth Street, the site was occupied by buildings for Time & Life (the magazine publishers), Eastern Air Lines, and the United States Rubber Company. Here the blockiness of the Associated Press Building was countered by the slab of Time & Life, thirty-six stories with a narrow face on Forty-ninth Street but running back to Forty-eighth Street along the whole eastern side of the Rockefeller Plaza block. Erected without a trace of setback, it was permitted to achieve its effect under the city's zoning laws because it does not come out to the building line.

While these buildings were being pushed, but not to the point of beginning excavation except for Time & Life, a minor revolution took place in the Rockefeller Center management. Since the beginning, this had been in the hands of a group of five managing agents chosen from among the seniors of the Todd, Robertson, Todd Engineering Corporation and Todd & Brown, with Robertson as the chief. During the depths of the Depression and in the early aftermath, the

Nelson A. Rockefeller (1932) congratulates one of 27 workers on the British Empire Building (Frank Spor, an elevator constructor) selected by their fellows as outstanding craftsmen. Their reward: a certificate and a gold button from the New York Building Congress.

progress of the work had been exemplary. But by 1936 the initial drive had leveled off.

Under the terms of their agreement as it then stood, each of the five managing agents received a salary topping that of all but a handful of major corporation presidents, as reported by the Internal Revenue Department of those days. One attempt to supplement or replace them with an executive committee of Rockefeller Center executives had failed. But the Center was losing money at the rate of $4 million a year. It could not hope to wipe out the deficit until all of the projected fourteen buildings were rented. Obviously, that could not come about while four of them, still not built, remained in a planning stage, which meant the last would not be finished until well into the 1940's.

Nelson Rockefeller, who had wound up his own brokerage

business and was now taking an increasingly active part in Center planning and operations, thinks the job never would have been finished if left to what he scornfully calls "management by committee." He believes that his was the major influence in persuading his father to terminate the managing agent agreement, which was soon to expire anyway. The senior Rockefeller was not only persuaded, he appointed Nelson to be executive vice-president of the Center in July, 1937, shortly after his twenty-ninth birthday, and president the next year. Robertson was named executive manager with the exercise of major but not supreme operational duties. The new buildings were opened one a year to 1940, by which time Rockefeller Center was not exactly making money but no longer had an operating deficit nor did it need the regular infusions from Rockefeller's checkbook.

The most important result of the change was that it put the active managment of the project in the hands of the next generation of the family and the men they selected. Nelson thinks that this is what ensured the continuation of his father's policy of that extra 5 percent to guarantee excellence. It is doubtful that, in the immediate situation, others would have been as determined to maintain it.

This was the year, 1937, when the word "recession" was applied to the nation's economy, a much less frightening expression than "crash" or "panic." But business was falling off as much as if people were using the harsher terms. Suggestions to cut corners in quality were offered freely to Rockefeller Center's new management, and they were declined. The young executive vice-president was urged to leave the three remaining sites vacant, for excavation had not been begun on any of them. But neither father nor son wanted to stop now; young Rockefeller pushed the construction as fast as he could—saving some money, too, in another year of declining prices—and his father continued to sign checks.

10

"As Beautiful as Possible"

Few palaces, seats of government, or religious institutions have been built with as much concern for artistic embellishment as was lavished assiduously on Rockefeller Center. Painting, sculpture, landscaping, photography, and lighting have been employed in profusion. Almost every form and technique one can think of is represented somewhere about the place. There is something to delight every taste, and probably no man would delight in everything.

Architecture, of course, is the Center's basic art, and in architecture it has made its most profound artistic impression, as has been indicated by both its admirers and its critics. But at least as much praise and blame have been directed at the decoration inside and out.

Such decoration was part of the original concept, but it had to wait for the main buildings to take form before it could be planned in any detail. Then, in 1932, an Advisory Art Committee began the task that has accumulated more painting and sculpture than many a large city museum can boast. The next year outdoor landscaping was started, including some which has been favorably compared to the hanging gardens of Babylon by authorities who talk as if they had seen both. Certainly, a great many people took seriously the admonition to make the project "as beautiful as possible."

It started in May, 1932, with a search for an appropriate theme. H. B. Alexander, a University of Southern California professor of philosophy, was engaged to provide one, and he came up with "New Frontiers." The ideas embodied in this phrase were further refined by three eminent scholars, the presidents of Dartmouth College and the Rockefeller Foundation, and Professor Michael Pupin, Columbia's and perhaps the nation's foremost physicist. From all this emerged the conclusion, as nearly as it is remembered now, that the guiding principle in planning all Rockefeller Center decorative work should be the progress of man.

Meanwhile, the architects agreed among themselves to a recommendation. They had omitted from their designs so many of the stone curlicues which normally adorned office buildings in those days that they thought they should be entitled to say how the money saved ought to be spent. They wanted it used for good modern painting and sculpture. While Rockefeller did not commit himself to just this bargain, he did set aside a million dollars, as Harrison recalls, for art, a tremendous figure for that time—it would have paid for a hundred major works by the highest-priced artists alive.

An Advisory Art Committee was then appointed to recommend artists for commissions and to pass upon finished jobs. This committee consisted of a substantial bloc of the top formal esthetic hierarchy in America, leading experts from art museums in Philadelphia, Boston, and New York and the

Yale University School of Fine Arts. It prepared and conducted several competitions that resulted in works installed
at the Center. But the members, not among the foremost
authorities on contemporary artists, were in fact especially
weak when it came to modern painting. However, it is not
clear that they had much to do with many phases of the art
program. Certainly, they were innocent bystanders in what
was the principal art controversy of Rockefeller Center and,
for that matter, of the decade.

The outstanding location for a dominant mural painting
was the wall facing the main entrance of the RCA Building,
and only a little less important were the walls to either side.
The architects wanted Matisse and Picasso for the side walls
and Diego Rivera, to represent the Americas, for the front
wall. Matisse and Picasso declined offers of a commission but
Rivera accepted. José Maria Sert of Paris and Sir Frank
Brangwyn of London were then engaged to do the others.

The choice of Rivera was largely that of Mrs. John D.
Rockefeller, Jr., whose taste ran to the moderns. He had
painted portraits of her grandchildren, and she owned several
of his other works. She was ardently abetted in her selection
by her son Nelson, but one doubts if the Art Advisory Committee, if consulted, was enthusiastic.

It so happened that Rivera was almost as well known for
his Communist views, which had not always been considered
strictly orthodox in Moscow, as for his depiction of the Mexican scene. As a revolutionary in politics and art, he was delighted to be entrusted with the central mural of a project
that would express "New Frontiers" or the progress of man.
He was not long in submitting a suggestion. He proposed to
show intelligence in possession of the forces of nature on one
side of his mural and the workers of the world inheriting the
earth on the other side. This was approved. He followed with
a sketch which was a standard Marxian interpretation of the

theme, but so illuminated by touches of his own genius that
Nelson Rockefeller, the Center's authority on modern art,
was enthusiastic.

In this sketch, the central figure—a "worker's leader" in
Rivera's phrase—was drawn as an anonymous, unidentifiable
man in a cloth cap. So, too, he appeared in outline on the
wall itself when Rivera and a small army of assistants began
to translate the sketch into a mural. Rivera was working in
fresco, painting directly on the plaster, whereas the Sert and
Brangwyn murals were being painted on canvas in the artists'
studios to be shipped to the United States when finished.

At the end, Rivera and his helpers had to work feverishly
to complete his fresco in time for the formal inauguration, set
for a little later in May than the actual opening for business.
It became a favorite pastime for those who could get in to
run up to Rockefeller Plaza to view the progress of the
work.

Early in the spring there began to be indignant comments
in the newspapers. The mural obviously was repeating, not
very subtly, the even then stereotyped Communist views of the
United States and its society. Gambling and venereal disease,
represented by female figures not remotely resembling any in
Rivera's original sketch, occupied prominent positions. Jin-
goes in the press were caustic about Rockefellers who pro-
moted or permitted this sort of propaganda. Lesser outcries
were raised against those who urged interference with an
artist. The Rockefellers themselves were restive but silent.

Whether they might have attempted to persuade the
painter to modify the crudities of his message no one now can
be sure. For the mural at the last minute plunged into a
sharper controversy.

Rivera was under pretty severe pressure, if only from himself. He was not yet ready to disregard the Soviet rulers of
Stalinism, as he would be a few years later when he welcomed

Leon Trotsky and gave him a refuge in Mexico. He knew that his Mexican revolutionary views were considered suspect in Moscow, and he felt he had to prove himself. Thirty years later, his friend and biographer, Bertram D. Wolfe, wrote: "The fact that he was painting for a Rockefeller and that the Communist Party was attacking him as a painter for millionaires strengthened his determination to show what a good Communist he was.

Wolfe thought that the patron … had been thoroughly … himself as to the intention … he artist." But even he … the impression that he was su…rised by one major de… in the execution of that intention…n. As the mural neared completion it was apparent that the … "worker's leader" was undergoing revisions. First, he mer…y lost his cap. Since he was almost the face began to recei…recognizable features, it was only a few days before the sch…uled inauguration that the 'worker's leader' was seen to … Lenin, bald, bearded, almost a replica of the portrait with … hung in every Russian home and office. Furthermore, it de…inated the whole paint-…ing … Wolfe says.

Managed … but pre…served its equanimity, leaving to Nelson Rockefeller the job of bringing the painter …ession. He wrote on May 4

While I was in the Number 1 building at Rockefeller Center yesterday viewing the progress of your thrilling mural, I noticed that in the most recent portion of the painting you had included a portrait of Lenin. This piece is beautifully painted but it seems to me that the portrait, appearing in this mural, might very easily seriously offend a great many people. If it were in a private house it would be one thing, but this mural is in a public building and the situation is therefore quite different. As much as I dislike to do so I am afraid we must ask you to substitute the face of some unknown man where Lenin's face now appears.

You know how enthusiastic I am about the work which you

have been doing and that to date we have in no way restricted you in either subject or treatment. I am sure you will understand our feeling in this situation and we will greatly appreciate your making the suggested substitution.

Meetings with the artist failed to budge him. On May 6 Rivera replied in writing that he would not change the portrait. He asserted that the head of Lenin had been included in his original sketch although only "as a general and abstract representation of the concept of leader." He went on:

Moreover, I understand quite thoroughly the point of view concerning the business affairs of a commercial public building, although I am sure that the class of person who is capable of being offended by the portrait of a deceased great man, would feel offended, given such a mentality, by the entire conception of my painting. Therefore, rather than mutilate the conception, I should prefer the physical destruction of the conception in its entirety, but preserving, at least, its integrity.

Seldom has a difference of opinion between patron and painter exploded with such widespread and furious repercussions. To the small band of American Communists, probably fewer than 30,000 members at that time, but with more sympathizers and followers as a result of the Depression, was added the highly vocal army of artists and liberals who thought esthetic honor and free expression were at stake. Neither the Soviet Union nor the American Communist Party was regarded as being nearly the threat to the United States Government that they became later. Therefore, the heat of the controversy was not lessened by any fear of those who took Rivera's part that they might be penalized as subversive.

The painter himself once came close to making the perfect analogy, although his unfamiliarity with the Italian Renaissance and its leading figures led his reasoning astray. He suggested that it was as if an American millionaire bought the Sistine Chapel containing the work of Michelangelo.

"Would that millionaire have the right to destroy the Sistine Chapel?" he demanded, and of course he was answered with a universal roar of "No."

As a Communist, even if Moscow did not so regard him, Rivera did not concede any difference between the Vatican and Rockefeller Center, between the Medici of the sixteenth century and the Rockefellers of today. And he was not quite Michelangelo either, a point which could easily have escaped a proud man.

In truth, however, his comparison would have been valid if he had imagined the great Florentine trying to insert a recognizable portrait of Martin Luther in his masterpiece "The Last Supper." To a student of history, the idea of Michelangelo rejecting an artistic suggestion from either Pope Leo X or Clement VII, son and nephew of his revered first patron, Lorenzo the Magnificent, is inconceivable. But assume that he was capable of insisting on putting Luther's portrait into the Sistine Chapel, imagination boggles at contemplating the fate a Medici, or any Pope of the era, would have devised for so rash an artist. Admirers of Michelangelo can hardly escape the feeling that the Mexican might have made a better case if he had selected another example from the history of art.

However, few of the passionate controversialists in 1933 appealed to the past. Either you were sure Rivera was a villain seeking to impose dangerous alien propaganda upon the innocent or you thought the Rockefellers the embodiment of capitalist evil, seeking to dictate to a free artist. Hardly anyone took the calm, objective middle ground of Will Rogers, the cowboy wit who was the day's most popular and in some respects most profound commentator on the passing scene. At this lapse of time, the angry recriminations of the most eloquent participants are unintelligible, but Rogers' comment, dated May 15, sums it all up admirably:

I am hereby entering the argument between young Rockefeller

and the Mexican artist, for there are two things that a dumb guy knows as much about as a smart one, and that's art and inflation.

I string with Rockefeller. This artist was selling some art and sneaking in some propaganda. Rockefeller had ordered a plain ham sandwich, but the cook put some onions on it. Rockefeller says, 'I will pay you for it, but I won't eat the onions.'

Now the above is said in no disparagement of the Mexican artist, for he is the best in the world, but you should never try to fool a Rockefeller in oils.

Maybe you could not fool him, but you could make it pretty hard for him to decide what to do with these particular oils. Inauguration day for the RCA Building came, and the ceremonies passed off with the Rivera mural shrouded conspicuously under canvas. It remained so covered for nine months because Rockefeller Center did not want to take the painter at his word. Rather than remove the painting out of hand, which would demolish it forever, they waited and hoped that he would yield. As Rogers said, they had paid his full fee of $21,500, handsome for the time. At last, no agreement seeming possible, the mural was destroyed to the accompaniment of a renewed flare-up in which the Rockefeller Center management was damned on one side as a bunch of vandals and on the other, for waiting so long to treat the Red wretch as he deserved. The fresco was replaced by another Sert canvas, "American Progress." This is as noncontroversial a work by a fine artist as you are likely to see; if you can identify anybody's portrait, it probably is Lincoln or Edison.

One tangible result of the Rivera incident survived. His fee left him a surplus to finance painting the mural all over again with unimportant propaganda changes, but not up to the original fresco artistically, his admirers have said. He did it on twenty-one moveable mural panels and called it "Portrait of America." Originally housed in the New Workers

School in New York, eighteen of them were moved to the International Ladies Garment Workers Union's Camp Unity in Pennsylvania. The other three, which Wolfe thinks the union considered "perhaps too overtly Communistic," found their way to the home of a private collector.

A war and a recession later, Nelson Rockefeller, looking back at the furore with the hindsight of a decade and a half, remarked: "It was eight years before he would even speak to me again. But we're good friends now."

Nothing about the adornment of Rockefeller Center—and much was added as new buildings went up—ever approached this incident in excitement and publicity, and the management is not sorry. The nearly two hundred other works of art by almost fifty artists, including many of the world's best known and most highly regarded, can be looked at calmly for what they are. Outside of a few museums and government building complexes, this is the most important collection of contemporary art in the country. Besides the oils, there is sculpture and carving in stone, bronze, wood, stainless steel, aluminum, and glass. Mosaics, photography, gilding, and enameling have been used. The roster of artists, in addition to the ones already mentioned, includes Paul Manship, Carl Jennewein, Lee Lawrie, Naum Gabo, Isamu Noguchi, Ezra Winter, Alfred Janniot, Fritz Glarner, Dean Cornwell, Carl Milles, Joseph Albers, and Giacomo Manzu.

Unusual materials or techniques make some of these works interesting to read about as well as to see. For the main entrance of the RCA Building, facing Rockefeller Plaza, Lee Lawrie designed limestone panels and a glass screen for the lintels of the three arches over the doorways. The figures represent Wisdom, with Light on one side and Sound on the other, an appropriate inspiration for a broadcasting center. The glass screen, fifty-five feet by fifteen, is 240 blocks and thirteen tons of glass cast in eighty-four molds.

Paul Manship's Prometheus presides over the Rockefeller Center skating pond as spectators look on from Rockefeller Plaza above. The flags are part of the United Nations display.

Another unusual use of glass is at the building's opposite entrance on what is now called the Avenue of the Americas, once Sixth Avenue, where Barry Faulkner created a seventy-nine foot by fourteen mosaic of "Intelligence Awakening Mankind" with about a million bits of glass enameled in more than 250 colors.

In the Lower Plaza, for which no definite use had been devised at the time, Manship's gilded bronze statue of a Prometheus eighteen feet tall was erected to preside over a fountain (which jokers once animated with detergent to watch the foam) backed by a quotation from Aeschylus carved in a red Balmoral granite wall. After fifteen years, the statue, one of the most photographed pieces of sculpture in the world, began to look shabby as most city sculpture that is kept outdoors, and so it was regilded. The process was repeated in 1958, an interval of only eleven years, so perhaps the city gets dirtier. It takes a trained crew three weeks, working inside a temporary airtight shelter built over the whole statue, to apply more than a pound of gold leaf.

Manship's mythology was not universally comprehended in the early days. A Robert Day cartoon in *The New Yorker* summed up the philistine view. It depicted two timid elderly ladies, dwarfed by the giant Prometheus, asking a guard, "Pardon me, but is this to be permanent?"

For all the fun people had with it, Prometheus became a symbol of Rockefeller Center and a favorite of the public. When he was twenty-five years old, in May of 1958, an animated color curtain was created as a backdrop for him. Fifty new jets of water played upon by electronically controlled beams of colored light give a twelve-minute show which has been put on every summer evening at intervals from dusk to 1 A.M. After the first year, synchronized music on tape was added to provide a symphony of both sound and color. Nowadays, timid, elderly ladies perhaps just hope it will be permanent.

Less sport has been made of the other Center example of heroic sculpture, Lawrie's bronze statue of Prometheus' big brother Atlas, outside the International Building's entrance on Fifth Avenue. He is a conventional Atlas, fifteen feet tall on a nine-foot pedestal, supporting on his shoulders a twenty-one foot sphere. But instead of the usual solid globe, this sphere is in the form of a set of open rings with the signs of the zodiac in the outermost ring.

Noguchi, a young Los Angeles sculptor who had been a student of both Borglum and Brancusi, won the Center's $1,000 prize for the entrance panel of the Associated Press Building, "News." His design was the first piece of heroic sculpture ever cast in stainless steel. Another unusual use of metal is the "constructivist" bas relief in the United States

Rubber Company Building, executed in aluminum, plastic, and a special alloy, phosphor-bronze. The artist, Gabo, has said simply that "it represents the image of itself."

A return to the more conventional and classical (and intelligible) has marked the latest in the Rockefeller Center art collection, a set of new bronze doors for the Palazzo d'Italia, executed by Italy's Giacomo Manzu. They were unveiled in May, 1965, at a ceremony in which David Rockefeller called the artist "one of the great sculptors of our time" and noted that the doors, given to the Center by the Fiat Company, were the first of Manzu's work to be on public display in America. The high relief is an entwined grapevine and wheat stalks to symbolize fruitfulness. The bas relief is an immigrant mother and child, looking the part besides being beautiful.

A mural in the outer office of the president of Rockefeller Center, Inc., shows what Columbia's Upper Estate looked like in the nineteenth century, rather idealized since it includes both Dr. Hosack's greenhouse and some of the post-War Between the States brownstones on the avenue. In the International Building on the Rockefeller Plaza side, two limestone panels by Gaston Lachaise represent wreckers clearing the site and steelworkers being hoisted aloft on a girder.

The unexpectedly lovely gardens are one Rockefeller Center beautifying effort for which few have had anything but praise. There are a lot of them, in the upper and lower plaza, on the roofs and in bits of additional landscaping such as trees on the streets or patches of shrubbery and flowers around an entrance. Perhaps no other similarly urban building complex has anything like the amount, richness, and variety of these; few other commercial enterprises have tried.

The original opera plans had called for a plaza with gar-

Some of the roof gardens as they actually materialized. These are seven stories above Fifth Avenue, looking south from 51st Street. From front to back they are the gardens of the International Building North, Palazzo d'Italia, British Empire Building and La Maison Francaise.

dens and fountains, and although nobody in modern times had included such frills among privately owned office buildings, the concept never was abandoned here. It was not even diminished in any of the multitude of detailed proposals that were examined seriously.

The idea of putting the hanging gardens of Babylon in the shade was an added starter, originating with Raymond Hood. Before there were any setbacks or low buildings to provide roofs to be turned into gardens, he proposed what in effect was a modern version of Dr. Hosack's dream. It is much harder to find fault with a flower than with a painting or sculpture, although Mumford would sneer that the "hanging

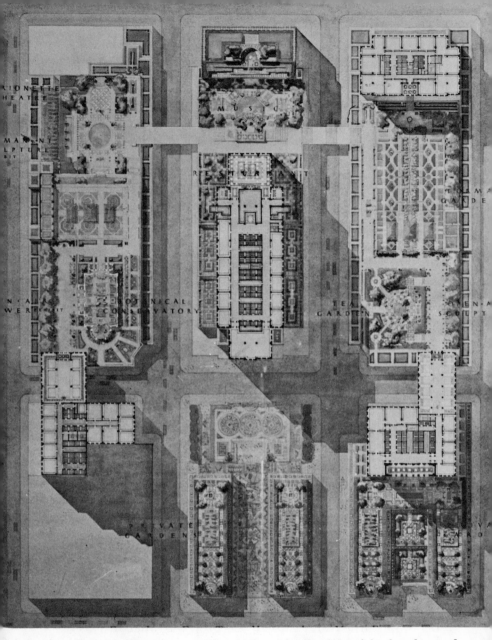

One of the early renderings (that of John Wenrich) for the roof gardens. It dates from the period when a second-story promenade with walks elevated over the cross streets was still in the mind's eye.

gardens give the effect, from the street, of inverted mistakes," so Hood's suggestion was unanimously acclaimed. The final achievement outdid his early concept. The gardens at one time were some four times as spacious as Babylon's and nearly one quarter of the acreage originally leased from Columbia.

These gardens had to defy both the city and the heights on which they perch. Midtown Manhattan's air is not what it was in Hosack's day, and it has been getting progressively less healthy for vegetation ever since the wreckers and excavators destroyed the last remnants of backyard planting on the site. There are problems of altitude, too. Plants which thrive at ground level, even amid the exhaust fumes, die ten floors up, but one can select Alpine types which prefer the high winds. Eventually, the casualties and costs were so great that the roof gardens shrank to about half their maximum acreage.

Trees have been the greatest horticultural headache. English elms were planted first, for they are a traditional curbside selection. They were unable to survive the detritus that washes into downtown New York soil and the polluted air that their leaves have to breathe. Then American elms were tried, apparently in the hope that they would be able to deal with the peculiarly American atmosphere. They died even faster; not even special injections of food and medicine could save them.

Finally it was discovered that honey locusts could make it; they are in the botanical kingdom like a man whose health endures constant exposure to the air in nightclubs. The first honey locusts planted were fifty feet tall with balls of earth ten feet in diameter around their roots. Elaborate access holes for watering and feeding were installed. For all this care, an occasional tree still dies and has to be replaced, more often than the plane trees which seem to do all right on the side streets.

At one point the whole tree policy was reviewed. Best & Company, a department store for women, moved to the east said of Fifth Avenue at Fifty-First Street, and it was suggested that this firm also plant some trees.

"Trees should have no place on Fifth Avenue," the president of Best replied sharply, and he was roundly criticized for lack of civic virtue.

Rockefeller Center, grateful for being left out of one esthetic controversy in the neighborhood, took another look at itself and decided trees had come to stay.

One gardening venture proved overly ambitious. A Horticultural Hall was built on the roof of the tenth floor of the RCA Building adjoining a three-quarter-acre Garden of Nations. Both were operated by a leading garden authority, Ralph Hancock, who installed and for a time cared for all the Rockefeller Center gardens. The enterprise did not work out financially despite space rented in the Hall to nurserymen, landscapers, and the like, and a dollar admission charge to the Garden of Nations. Hancock had to give it up.

The man who made the gardens the attraction they are today was Hancock's successor, a delightful Hollander named Aart Marius Van den Hoek, who took over in 1938. Naturally he introduced bulbs from his native land, but during his dozen years as director, he ranged over the whole horticultural world to get the effects he wanted.

While the roof gardens attract the imagination, the flower beds at ground level attract the visitors, and by the millions every year. Perhaps the most spectacular ones, are those in the Channel Gardens.

Decorating a broad promenade leading to the lower plaza, six beds are accented by six granite fountain pools. The fountainheads are bronze tritons and nereids riding on the backs of dolphins toward a skating pond below, and are said to symbolize qualities of leadership, will, thought, imagination,

The Channel Gardens during July and August, looking west from Fifth Avenue. The beds are planted with hibiscus, red and white caladiums and lantana of many colors. Lilies and other blooming aquatic plants adorn the pools. In the background are some of the United Nations flags and the RCA Building entrance.

energy, and alertness. That may even be so; what is obvious is that they are spirited and attractive figures. They were executed by René Chambellan who, despite his name, came from Hoboken, New Jersey. Even when the gardens are without blossoms from November to April, the promenade retains grace and color.

Rockefeller Center's series of major floral displays begin here each April with masses of Easter lilies. People have come to expect the traditional on this occasion, and when some lover of innovation decided to introduce calla lilies too one year, a lot of grumbling was heard. "Not a real Rockefeller Center Easter," muttered one elderly gentleman morosely.

Tulips follow the lilies, and every few weeks come another of eight more replacements, ending up with chrysanthemums in October. The channel has been known to use as many as 150 varieties of flowers in a year, and about 20,000 separate plants. A few years ago a more modest series of displays was begun a block up Fifth Avenue, the flowers being set out in boxes around the base of the Atlas statue. In order to have plants in bloom on the date they are desired, the orders are placed a year ahead of time with growers who specialize in each variety.

Newer parts of the Center are planned to keep up with the floral tradition and have done almost as much as new building to change the aspect of the Avenue of the Americas. There evergreens around the pools of the Time & Life Building are a splash of color in winter, replaced with flowers in spring. These are supplemented by several displays changed for the seasons in the large beds of the Sperry Rand Building.

To those who take care of all this, at least to John Buckley, a Center gardener for many years, this display caters to two categories of visitors. Buckley used to say that there were only those who asked for advice and those who gave it.

One more decorative feature of Rockefeller Center seemed for a time to be getting out of hand, and it may do so yet. In the late 1940's, it was suggested that the flags of each of the United Nations members fluttering from poles along the esplanade around the lower plaza would make a brave display of color. So, beginning with the setting out of the Easter lilies, until Thanksgiving, the flags are flown every day the weather permits. In 1950 this meant sixty flags, which was quite a lot but manageable. Sixteen years later there were 117, and handling that many can be quite a problem.

One of the perils is the chance that something like the incident of the irate Arab would be repeated. There are people at Rockefeller Center today who shudder if you remind them of the day this gentleman turned up at the main information desk of the RCA Building across the street from the United Nations display. He was in a state of vociferous outrage and succeeded in creating quite a scene. It seems the flag of Saudi Arabia had been hung upside down. The Center's succinct file on the subject simply notes: "Patrolman detailed to correct condition." The Arab's remarks are deleted.

Through the many ramifications of Rockefeller Center's art collection, it is hard to see any central, unifying thread except the genuine intention to heed that first admonition, "as beautiful as possible." But whose concept of beauty? Certainly not that of he who paid the bills. Maybe, in addition to the Gothic railing nobody but he can see, the ornamental motif in the spandrels over the window bays in the earliest group of buildings represents his taste, although his son Nelson thinks these were just "Father's concession to the reactionary element."

Apparently, behind the scenes esthetic arguments within the circle of the Center's executives and advisers were as keen as any outside, although conducted with better humor and less recrimination. Nor was the final decision on a given point necessarily determined by the exponent's rank in the hierarchy. The man at the very top set the tone of restraint in the exercise of authority in these matters, and so no one imposed his will all the time.

In some instances one seems to see the modern, sophisticated style of Nelson Rockefeller or Wallace Harrison. Again, the more conservative taste of Hugh Robertson or Dr. James Todd or—in the Music Hall—of Roxy is in evidence. And often, one suspects, there was a compromise between two or more.

Out of it all has come a curiously practical conclusion. The many millions of dollars spent on beautifying the place— Rockefeller Center probably could compile a fairly exact total figure, but has never bothered to do so—were spent in line with what Mr. Junior conceived as a civic responsibility. But they have proved a sound business investment as well. Beauty on this scale, it turns out, is reflected in a nice upward trend in the price per square foot that can be asked for office space.

11

Cool, Clean, and Collected

One night not so long ago a member of the staff of 1,178 cleaners who keep Rockefeller Center from succumbing to the common New York blight of dust and soot got as far in her regular routine as the private washroom of an RCA Building tenant on the twenty-ninth floor. The door's throw-bolt jammed, and when a guard finally heard her it took an hour to get her out. A panel had to be removed from the door by unscrewing the moulding.

Involved besides the cleaning woman and the guard were a carpenter who took the panel out and put it back, a lock-smith who repaired the bolt, a painter who touched up the door after the others were through, and a man at the Center's massive control board who logged the incident for posterity. They were all available within the Center's walls because maintenance of such a place requires the constant attention of skilled men and women in almost every craft you can think of.

Just the housekeeping alone has been estimated as the equivalent of cleaning eight thousand six-room houses every day. Dusting—women for everything up to shoulder height, men above that—scrubbing, waxing, polishing, cleaning carpets, and washing windows are routine, but on a scale which has led to a mass of statistics fascinating to people who do not have to do the dirty work.

Every year Rockefeller Center uses up 62,000 pounds of cleaning agents or detergents, 48,000 pounds of rags and dusters, and 18,000 pounds of waxes and polishes. The task of washing 31,068 windows is continuous in order to get at each once a month—it was a big job to count them, let alone clean them. One hundred men and women are needed every night at the Music Hall after the last show to get the place ready for next day; they empty 2,700 ashtrays, for example.

The chores are onerous enough even when the staff understands its instructions. That does not always happen. One new porter assigned to RCA Building elevators was told to clean the "Sixth Avenue cabs." He nodded and disappeared. After a frustrating search, his foreman located him outside on the Avenue of the Americas industriously sweeping out the taxis parked along the curb while their admiring drivers watched.

Just collecting the trash and getting rid of it is a carefully plotted campaign. Two hundred thousand people, nearly a quarter of them working in the center's shops and offices, would create a mess even if they were all tidy. They are not. They have been known to throw plastic catsup containers out of windows, set fire to telephone books in the lobbies, misplace fish, and (in one of the foreign consulates) try to burn up top secret papers in the wastebasket. So every day truckloads of refuse accumulate.

The simplest method of disposal would be to truck it away

as fast as it is collected. But people are not only untidy, they are careless. Running an office building complex on this scale calls for some care in retaining the trash until the tenants have a chance to discover what they threw away by mistake. In Rockefeller Center, jewelry, watches, and valuable papers make up the bulk of the items retrieved from the trash. The recoveries also have included $80,000 worth of diamonds tossed into a jewelry store wastebasket, $20,000 in negotiable bonds dropped in an elevator and swept up by the porter who cleaned it, a $12,000 check in a letter posted by a clerk in the rubbish can instead of the mailbox, a good-sized unset diamond picked up with the dust from a diamond cutter's floor and found in the vacuum cleaner bag.

A routine which permits such finds without unbearably shackling the workers has been devised. All wastepaper, about 1,300 big bags of it every day, goes to a paper manufacturer who holds it for twenty-four hours. The vacuum cleaners for each building are emptied into a separate bin and the contents kept until next evening, so a reported loss can be traced.

There is no complete substitute for what used to be known as human elbow grease for cleaning. That is why, in spite of all the modern advances blazoned on television, and a lot that are not because they are bigger than household size, the Rockefeller Center cleaning staff rose from 630 in the 1930's to 850 in the 1950's to nearly 1,200 in the 1960's. But the automatic and other improved machinery, new cleaners, and polishers have made the task simpler and easier, sometimes safer. Built-in tracks on which window washers move up and down and around the outside of new buildings obviate the necessity for going through every office in the place. A two-man team operating a portable flash boiler takes up chewing gum neatly and quickly from floors and sidewalks where porters used to spend hundreds of hours on their knees with a razor blade. But it still has to be removed by hand, twenty pounds of it a day on the average, from under the 6,200 seats of the Music Hall. New machines replace a lot of manual work done in the 1930's in the way of polishing marble, bronze, and floors.

Special techniques have to be applied to works of art, and here even the specialists can be stumped. One crisis which sent the Center's management into a mild dither some years ago was the thick coat of dust and dirt which accumulated on the sculptured wood mural "Man and Nature" in the build-ing now named for General Dynamics. It is one of the most popular in the Center, partly because it is nice to look at but also because one small figure in it, a singing bird in a tree, actually moves its wings and warbles a nightingale's tune once an hour. It was the work of Carl Milles, the Swedish artist who became an American in 1945 and lived in Michi-gan. He had carved the mural out of the pine of his adopted state.

Since the cleaning experts were undecided as to the proper method of removing the dirt, they wrote to Milles to find out. His reply, by air mail and four pages long, was an anguished howl of outrage. He was furious that anyone should so much as think of anything that might disturb the precious patina of age on his mural. He threatened legal action and physical violence against man or woman who dared do it. Then, having somewhat exhausted his indignation, he suggested that the experts might see if they could blow the dust off with a bellows. It worked; a bellows has been added to the bat-teries of cleaning paraphernalia at the Center, and "Man and Nature" preserves its patina.

Of all the revolutions which have taken place in large-scale housekeeping of this kind since Rockefeller Center opened, the most important has been air conditioning. It is, of course, a revolution in comfort, too, and more important to the

tenants on that account. And it has been made largely during
the lifetime of Rockefeller Center.

Before and during the Depression, air conditioning was
largely confined to theaters, restaurants, a few special industrial facilities, and occasional homes of plutocrats. Only when
it became common in office buildings was it apparent that
one of the advantages of never opening a window was that
soot and dust get in much less, especially when the building
could be built for the process in the beginning with an airtight "skin" and windows which not only did not open but
could not.

The center went in so heavily for air conditioning from
the start that it has been credited in some real estate circles as
having been a pioneer. (That is not quite exact. The Egyp-
tians used it 4,000 years earlier.) When in 1901 Andrew
Carnegie moved into his new eighty-eight-room mansion on
Fifth Avenue and Ninetieth Street (later the home of the
New York School of Social Work), it was air-conditioned
throughout (except for the servants' quarters on the top
floor) with a separate electrical control in each room. But
Rockefeller Center did promote the practice of making this
comfort available for ordinary office workers.

Its million-dollar contract with the Carrier Engineering
Corporation—Willis Carrier was the real founder of the industry in this country—was by far the largest written up to
then. Carrier completed the job in 1933, the year of the first
air-conditioned automobile and railroad car. The capacity of
2,692 tons in the Music Hall, British Empire Building, La
Maison Francaise, and parts of the RCA Building was by far
the largest in the world. Today, with the Center 100 percent
air-conditioned except for a few scattered tenants in the earlier buildings who do not especially care for it, the capacity is
32,823 tons. Buildings erected after World War II included it
in their construction as a matter of course.

During World War II no air conditioning could be installed anywhere. Afterward, the task became one of the first preoccupations of Eyssell when he came over from the Music Hall to be executive manager of the Center and then, in 1951, president. More than $12 million was allotted for the job; that buys a lot of air conditioning, but a lot was needed. Fortunately, the high ceilings, which had seemed so extravagant in the 1930's, made it possible to hide all the pipes and ducts above new, slightly lower ceilings. A good many tenants shared the cost; other offices were air-conditioned when vacated and before another tenant moved in. By the time the whole job was done, Rockefeller Center was as up-to-date in its first as in its latest buildings.

The whole mechanical revolution—new lighting, automatic elevators, faster and stronger machines—was accompanied by a distinct revolution in personnel, too, or rather in the role of personnel; the turnover of individuals was much less than in most such enterprises. From the very beginning, Rockefeller Center has had a peculiar relationship with its staff. Through several eras of acute labor problems and disputes in both the nation and the city, the Center has undergone only one walkout, and that was a wildcat strike of building and maintenance workers for a few days in 1943, brief enough that supervisory personnel were able to give a reasonable facsimile of service while it lasted.

The management's personnel policy was not strictly formulated until after the recession of 1937. Up to then, any union problems would have been largely those of the contractors. The Center's management had only some routine negotiations to cover a few members of the skilled trades hired for maintenance work. The porters, cleaning women, and elevator operators who were the bulk of the employees were not unionized at all. By adopting the simple and not really very expensive practice of paying as good wages and giving as good working conditions as existed anywhere else, the Center avoided any hint of trouble. There could be little doubt, however, that with the impetus the New Deal gave to unions generally, these workers were going to be organized sooner or later.

Rockefeller Center's policy on this point was dictated by the experience and the industrial relations philosophy of its owner. Rockefeller had been indoctrinated and his views shaped during one of the most famous—some say infamous—labor wars of the century. It took place, too, in a day when the word "war" was used advisedly. The conflict was the Colorado coal strike against the Rockefeller-dominated Colorado Fuel and Iron Company, and nineteen smaller firms as well, but they are hardly ever mentioned.

The strike, which lasted for fifteen months in 1913–14, was a bitter, bloody fight. It was also, as Rockefeller wrote to Fosdick years later, "one of the most important things that ever happened to the Rockefeller family." It is hardly too much to say that much of the way Rockefeller Center is run today stems from what Mr. Junior learned during the anxiety and doubts and humiliations of those months.

While the miners and their families, starving and freezing in makeshift homes in the hills, battled the militia and armed mine guards, the nation was discovering with disapproval that they were the victims of one of the least savory industrial setups in the land. The camps were run like feudal estates, with outsiders run off at gun point if they dared approach. There were not even any public rights of way through the towns, and schools and churches were operated and policed by the managers. Men lived in company shacks, shopped solely at company stores, paying prices the companies chose to fix, were denied the advantages of such state labor laws as existed, and were routinely cheated by the company hirelings who weighed the coal they mined. Of course, the public heard, too, that the managers insisted the men were perfectly contented, that only outside subversive, un-American agitators from the United Mine Workers of America stirred up trouble. But indignation was aroused by the news that since strikers were "trespassers" on private property, they had to take their families into tents exposed to the rigors of a Colorado winter.

The strike dragged on to the accompaniment of increasing but futile public outrage. For nearly eight months before, on a spring day, the militia stormed one of the tent colonies at a place called Ludlow, were resisted by miners with guns, and captured the colony after a sharp battle in which several men were killed. The troops triumphantly burned every shelter to the ground, and then it was discovered that they had also suffocated two women and eleven children in a cave. The public reaction to what is known in labor history as the Ludlow Massacre was explosive.

Some time before this John D. Rockefeller had turned over his controlling interest in the Colorado Fuel and Iron Company to his son. At forty, the son was considered still a young man in business, and he believed the reports he received from officers of the company. He also supported their contention that the whole thing was the evil work of agitators. But after the Ludlow Massacre he began to wonder if he had been well informed. Aides sent from New York to report convinced him that he had not, but by the time he could act on his new information the strike had at last been broken.

Meanwhile, he had enlisted the help of a Canadian Liberal leader and industrial relations expert, W. L. Mackenzie King, a future prime minister of his country. Between them they drew up a formula for labor peace which Rockefeller forced upon the officials of the Colorado Fuel and Iron Company, who felt that they had won the war and now were being deprived of the fruits of victory by an effete sentimentalist. Rockefeller insisted that the camps be brought back into the laws of the United States and made safe for citizens, even union organizers, to enter. He also created for the mines what have come to be called company unions but which the originators preferred to term employee representation plans.

In Colorado in 1915 this had been an advanced position for anyone aligned with employer interests, let alone for the man who employed the employers. In New York in the early 1930's it was more than most office building employees enjoyed. So when it was put into effect in Rockefeller Center at the end of 1934, it was satisfactory to the unorganized workers, so far as can be learned.

Within three years this ceased to be true. Representation was hardly an adequate tool for collective bargaining on equal terms. The value of unions was becoming clearer to the unorganized as they saw the solid benefits gained by millions in dozens of industries. So in 1938, the young executive vice-president, soon to be elevated to the presidency, decided to have the situation explored anew.

The explorer he chose was his younger brother, Winthrop Rockfeller. He came to the task with a background of various jobs, even as a common laborer in the Texas oil fields, a brief stint at the Chase Bank where he had felt as little at home as Nelson, and several months in the foreign trade department of the Socony-Vacuum Oil Company. He had developed an interest in, as he put it, "trying to find out more and more about the individual worker and his relations to his work, his family, and his community." So Nelson engaged him as an industrial relations consultant.

The suggestions he made in the form of a written report were a straightforward modernization of Mr. Junior's philosophy. It was clear, well-organized, and to the point. Winthrop recalls with a grin that his father seemed surprised that he had written it all by himself. It was a full recognition not only of the workers' right to present grievances and points of view, but of management's need to have that done. Yet Winthrop did not propose recognition of an outside union, to which he remained opposed. On that point he was overruled, but his way was somewhat eased. As he recounts it:

Nelson had been asked to be vice chairman of the Greater New York Fund, which was just being organized, the first joint money-raising campaign for the city's health and social agencies. He was too busy, and I guess he thought this was a good chance for his little brother to cut his teeth on a big job, so he suggested me, and I took it.

It turned out to be a full-time job, too, and he gave up his consultant's post.

The employee representation plan, which had given way in January, 1938, to an Independent Organization of Rockefeller Center Employees, was finished, and its successor lasted only a few months. It was recognized in a formal agreement signed in March but was taken over almost immediately by the American Federation of Labor's union of service workers, then called Building Maintenance Craftsmen. By the end of May, Rockefeller Center had signed a new agreement recognizing the Building Maintenance Craftsmen as sole bargaining agents for the Center's operating employees.

Labor problems did not automatically disappear. While no strikes developed, it became increasingly complicated to deal with the new union and also with all the craft unions represented in the various shops which kept the place going. In 1938, Nelson Rockefeller sought the help of a Dartmouth classmate who was a member of the General Motors public relations staff but had earlier achieved success in solving some tough personnel problems which a big taxicab company was having with those highly mercurial and individual fellows, the New York taxi drivers.

He was Victor Borella, a round-faced young New Englander, soft-spoken, amiable, and outgoing, but not really as gentle as he usually seemed. He realized that a new day had dawned in the relationship of unionized employees to management, and he had no reservations about welcoming it. He was one of those men who had the revolutionary notion that one secret of labor peace was the employer's willingness to see not only the employee's point of view but that of the union, too, and then try to give what was wanted within the framework of management's needs and rights. Borella is not defensive about this philosophy, which was as advanced in 1939 as Rockefeller's was in 1915. He made it work at Rockefeller Center in his successive posts as director of the personnel department, director of industrial relations, manager of operations, vice-president, and executive vice-president.

Labor peace has been kept, not without arguments but at least without work stoppages, through large and small disputes, except for that one wildcat strike. The delicate matter of elevator automation, which has often touched off long strikes by its threat of mass dismissals, was worked out in one of the early agreements to proceed with the mechanical automation only as fast as human attrition permitted. In other words, no one was fired, but men who quit, died, or retired were not replaced. The plan itself is not remarkable nor difficult to express, but it calls for a good deal of mutual confidence to make it work. Automation is often a serious stumbling block to labor peace elsewhere, largely because neither union nor employer trust each other.

Just as difficult at the Center was the negotiation over allowing one group of employees to leave and come back at will. They were the young men who took parties of visitors on guided tours of Rockefeller Center, and many of them were actors temporarily out of jobs. They wanted to take off a few weeks if offered a chance at a part, even for a short run.

They asked assurance of their jobs afterward or if the play flopped or if they were written out of the script. One of them was a tall, handsome fellow with an engaging manner named Gregory Peck, a very good guide. He quit over the issue, which reached a negotiating stage when steadier job holders protested against being "bumped" for returning actors. Then it became easy for young men to get better jobs or go into the Army and the Center switched to women.

Borella's favorite labor relations anecdote, however, concerns the revolt of the cleaning women. He tells it to illustrate the difference between the drab, shabby, rather pitiful "char" of fiction, or even the early days of the Center, and the competent, snappy professionals of today. He points out that modern office building standards demand more ability and higher wages than in the days when it was enough to have female derelicts or almost decrepit crones slop a little dirty water around with a mop and empty wastebaskets.

One of the terms of the union contract is that Rockefeller Center provide uniforms for the help. Wielders of dustcloth and sponge are very conscious of the lowly status accorded their type of employment, and they are not eager to be identifiable as scrubwomen as they proceed to and from work. Many of them wear their very best clothes into Rockefeller Center since they are going to change anyway.

This went well until the end of World War II released a great volume of textiles for civilian uses. The canny manufacturers, intent on finding new customers to replace the government, hit on the idea of encouraging women to use a lot more fabric in their costumes. Wartime styles had been patriotically skimpy. Why not cut loose, literally and figuratively?

Couturiers responded with the longest skirts seen in the memory of a lot of people. They called their innovation, or reversion, the "New Look." In the postwar prosperity, the cleaning women of Rockefeller Center were not to be denied. They lengthened their skirts stylishly and bought new slips. Naturally, they wore the long skirt and finest new slip to work. But when they donned their uniforms, the slips hung down several inches below the hem of the old-fashioned garments and, of course, got exceedingly dirty. Borella yielded to the storm of protest willingly, he explains, because it was not fair to make them buy two slips, and a thousand skirts were let down overnight to conform to current fashions.

As a city within a city, Rockefeller Center has its own police force or Scotland Yard, called in the management's organizational charts the Protection and Security Department. It performs just about all the functions of any police. It chases thieves and vandals, investigates losses, answers questions, and soothes lost children. It gets rid of undesirables (such as door-to-door salesmen), gives first aid to accident victims, balks suicides (mostly would-be jumpers from roofs or high windows), keeps traffic moving, questions suspicious loiterers (who may turn out to be impatient, nervous types waiting for their wives), and patrols the premises at night. It operates a lost-and-found department which collects and returns to owners misplaced crutches and parts of meat-slicing machines and mink stoles, besides the more usual wallets, umbrellas, sweaters, watches, cameras, handbags, eyeglasses and jewelry—three or four dozen on an average day. And at Rockefeller Center it also fights fires and releases tenants who lock themselves in at night.

Rockefeller Center has never had a serious fire, but plenty with enough smoke to cause scares. For years a special fire watch was maintained, but research into the actual conditions disclosed that 85 percent of all fires were reported by cleaners, so most of the special patrol was abolished.

The force was at its peak with 136 men in 1935; it hit a low of 80 in the 1950's and stands now at 83 uniformed guards and a handful of plainclothesmen, supervisors, and clerks. They do the job once performed by more in fewer buildings because of elaborate new equipment.

There has always been a complicated control board connected by fire alarms, burglar alarms, and telephones to every corner of the Center, manned twenty-four hours a day. More recently it has been supplemented by shortwave radio pagers. Rockefeller Center has its duly licensed transmitting station, KBS-260, at the control board so it can communicate with watchmen, plainclothesmen, night supervisory staff, porter foremen, electricians, and engineers. The log kept at the board is a record of just about everything that ever went wrong.

One example of a mishap that never did get recorded on the control board's log occurred during one of New York's major panics, a scare created by the "Mad Bomber" who scattered homemade bombs of pipe filled with explosive powder and a timer in telephone booths all around the city. He turned out to be a man who had a grudge against the Consolidated Edison Company. At the peak of the terror, Rockefeller Center's protection staff received a thorough briefing on the Mad Bomber, what sort of pipe he used, the appearance of his bombs as the police recreated them, and his strange predilection for telephone booths. Everyone was urged to be on the alert.

That night a member of the staff, who presumably had been dozing or daydreaming during the lecture, found a nice piece of pipe in a Center phone booth, left obviously by an absent-minded patron. It was just the kind and size the guard needed for a little do-it-yourself job at his home in a New Jersey suburb. He slipped the piece of pipe in his pocket and took it away. Promptly at nine o'clock the next morning, it blew up his kitchen. His co-workers thought it poetic justice that the blast completely ruined a fresh consignment of beer in his refrigerator.

Rockefeller Center is proud that such lapses are rare. It is also proud of its tenants; they are and always have been, Nelson Rockefeller says, of the blue chip variety. But still they do the strangest things.

There was this tourist office, for example—that of a foreign government, to be sure—that put some fish on display. When the display case's refrigeration system failed and the exhibit began to be noticeable to the human olfactory sense, someone simply removed it to a corner behind a bank of elevators where it smelled up that whole section of the building before porters followed their noses to it and took it away.

In the good old days before air conditioning was complete, the control board received a call that sounded like a flood emergency warning. It was actually a complaint that the rain was coming in a window. The girl on the board asked if the tenants had thought about closing the window. They had not.

As a sort of reverse twist to this one, passersby on the street were objecting to being spattered by water, and sometimes a darker fluid, when it was not raining. It turned out that employees of one of the major and bluest chip tenants were rinsing their coffee pot and blithely tossing the residues out of a thirty-story window. They were prevailed upon to use the wash basin.

Then arose the matter of tenants' cuspidors, a "crisis" of the year 1948. Borella, into whose domain such problems fall, was surprised to discover that there were a thousand or more cuspidors in the Center, none provided by the management. They seemed to proliferate in the offices of tobacco companies and the plushier rooms occupied by oil company tycoons who learned to chew in the field where smoking is forbidden in the neighborhood of wells. Cleaning women, flushed no doubt by their "New Look" victory, rebelled at emptying and polishing these containers. Peace was restored by assigning the task to men.

Of course, tenants have unexpected emergencies. One of the most bizarre was the arrival of a bat through an open RCA Building window—this was before the days of air conditioning. Where the bat came from, no one knows, but it hung upside-down on the ceiling of a large office and scared some of the girls there so much that work stopped completely. Eventually one of the Center's "high dusters" (men who clean office walls above the level women can reach) shooed the beast out through the window, and Rockefeller Center has not been bothered with bats since.

And then tenants lose keys. There are 84,750 locks in Rockefeller Center. One of the services maintained is a shop manned by five locksmiths. They keep busy changing and repairing locks and making new keys, of which there have been some five million in the Center's history, and attending to other bits of hardware. Tenants also need a lot of other services, and they use a considerable proportion of the time of the Center's fourteen carpenters, four masons, eight painters, and other assorted craftsmen, although more and more maintenance and service work is farmed out to independent contractors.

These and other even more essential mechanics for keeping the city within a city functioning properly are mostly well out of sight, anywhere from one to four floors below street level. Here in the bowels of the excavations are the huge pipes through which more than a billion pounds of steam, purchased formerly from the New York Steam Company and now from Consolidated Edison, comes in to heat the buildings, which were designed without furnaces of their own. Mains and pumps circulate the nearly half-billion gallons of water used each year. Motors, fans, generators, refrigerating equipment, recording devices for keeping track of the efficiency of the machines, more cables, pipes, and wires are part of the maze.

Rockefeller Center constructed the city's first comprehensive off-street truck space, and this takes up a lot of the subterranean room. Sometimes a thousand trucks a day drive down the ramps to the unloading platforms—most of the supplies are inbound—strategically placed to serve the various buildings. They would create an impossible traffic jam on the streets, and thirty-four feet underground their output of carbon monoxide could kill everybody in the place in a few minutes. Exhaust fumes, therefore, are sucked up through grilles and pipes to be blown out of ducts high above the surrounding streets. As new buildings were added, each was equipped with its own similar subterranean truck facility.

The value of the off-street truck delivery was so apparent immediately that the Center decided it might be sensible to get some of the passenger cars off the street, too. The first obstacle was New York's zoning regulations which forbade inclusion of a garage in an office building. Negotiations finally won a variance in 1938. Six floors of space above and below ground had been left for a garage in the Eastern Air Lines Building, then under construction as next to last of the original structures planned for the Center, and the last where a reservation had still been kept for the opera. Here room for seven hundred automobiles was provided early in 1939, an innovation for a New York office building.

Only recently has it become apparent that such facilities are necessary. When Rockefeller Center was begun, it was easy to find a place at the curb for a car almost anywhere in midtown New York; it was bad luck to have to walk half a block. But gradually the curbs filled up, and parking lots dotted the landscape; there had been one on the site of the new garage.

It was supposed that tenants would appreciate a place to park in the Center itself, even if they had to pay for the privilege, but in its first few years the garage was patronized

A garage attendant slides down one of the firemen's poles to retrieve a customer's car from a lower level.

mostly by shoppers and theater-goers who stored their cars for only several hours at a time, which was good business. Not until after World War II were the patrons business people who parked for eight or nine hours at a stretch, which still permits the place to handle about 1,200 cars a day. One of the recent improvements is a series of poles, copied from those in a firehouse, down which the garage's forty drivers slide with unflagging gusto to retrieve customers' cars. The first contingent learned the knack from a retired captain of the city's fire department—it is not as easy as it looks—and they have taught newcomers.

Most of all these assorted facilities, services, and problems exist because people work in Rockefeller Center. But the place has another aspect. A good many of the 160,000 visitors come for fun or at least for pleasure. And a good many of the men and women who work there cater to them.

12
Fun and Games

By the time the original block of buildings was finished in
1940, Rockefeller Center had become what it was originally
intended to be, an entertainment center. Of course, it was
not altogether in the form envisaged in 1928. Talking pictures had been only a year old then—the first was Al Jolson's
"The Jazz Singer"—and color was four years in the future,
coming in the year the Radio City Music Hall opened. Radio
had been the child prodigy of the performing arts, and television was a dream.

The development of these mass entertainment media had a
profound effect upon Rockefeller Center; the combination of
their influences helped to maintain the primacy of the Music
Hall among motion picture theaters, kill its smaller "intimate" sister, and almost double NBC's space in the RCA
Building to a mammoth eight hundred thousand square feet.
But the claim to fulfilling so much of the original objective

rests equally upon a great range of other facilities for public enjoyment. It is an impressive list, for it includes:

Outdoor ice skating in winter; dining and dancing in summer.

A small movie theater, the Guild of 450 seats, devoted to the unusual and artistic in feature films along with short subjects.

Four free museums and a myriad of special and temporary exhibitions of all kinds. The four at the time this book is written are Armstrong Cork's interior design display in a gallery of decorated room settings, incorporating ideas from all over the world; the Chase Manhattan Bank's Money Museum with items ranging from a five-thousand-year-old Babylonian clay tablet due bill to current coins and bills from many lands; the RCA Exhibition Hall with audience participation features, one of which permits the viewer to get the feel of space and another to see himself on television; the Time & Life Exhibition Center, featuring changing displays of art, graphics, and photography.

A number of radio and television performances to which the public is admitted, either as part of a studio audience or, as was for many years the case of the "Today Show," watching through the windows from the street where the camera picked up the scene and broadcast shots of visitors to their families back home.

Two restaurants featuring music, the Rainbow Grill on top of the RCA Building, called by *The New Yorker* "the tallest star in the firmament" because it is the highest up recreation place in town, and La Fonda del Sol on the ground level of the Time & Life Building.

One of the best views of New York and vicinity obtainable anywhere, this one from the Observation Roof of the RCA Building, seventy floors up.

The annual lighting and month-long display of perhaps the most famous Christmas tree in the world.

A guided tour of the Center generally, long ago denominated "Walk a Magic Mile."

All these put together are in a sense no more than the special attractions to spice the greatest and most general of all Rockefeller Center entertainments, just relaxing and looking around. Probably more people than ever attend the Music Hall watch the skaters on the Lower Plaza rink, stroll through the Channel Gardens, take a little time to admire or criticize some of the art, gape up at the towers, window shop in the concourse or on the street, come to stare at the Christmas tree, pause for some bit of music, oratory, festivity, or ceremony. The Center has become one of the world's major tourist attractions, and also about the nearest thing to a village green or community center that New York can boast.

Travel experts who should know say Rockefeller Center—all its attractions together, not just formal tours—outdraws anything else in the United States, including the Grand Canyon, the Statue of Liberty, and the Washington Monument. One proof of its lure for tourists is the story of the guided tours, the "magic mile" walked by well over half a million visitors a year. All day long every day, little groups of men, women, and children, not always out of towners, start from a lounge in the concourse and have a good look at wonders ranging from the truck delivery turn-around in the sub-basement to the observation roof. They are shepherded by attractive young women in Rockefeller Center uniforms, spiritual descendants of Dr. Hosack's gardeners who showed visitors around the grounds 160 years ago. The current guides explain, describe, and answer questions.

One question frequently asked, not of them but of officials of the Center, is who selects the girls and how. Another is whether the girls do not have a lot of trouble with unruly male charges.

The answer to the first is that they were selected by Maria Lombard, a woman who had thirty years of experience in screening applicants not only for trimness and neatness but for less obvious qualities, and she could spot just what she considered the right degree of warmth, intelligence, and poise that it takes to meet the public on such a job. Those who have fewer than two years of college and are more than twenty-six years old or less than twenty-one are weeded out. For the rest, personality will win over beauty if there is a contest because, as the management likes to say: "We want the girl to show off the Center, not the Center to show off the girl."

When the tours were first introduced, the guides were all young men. Up until World War II they did very well except for the problem of actors. Besides Gregory Peck, the famous alumni include Larry Parks and Thomas Merton, novelist, monk, and philosopher who wrote *Seven Story Mountain,* among other books. During the depression, young doctors, architects, and lawyers became guides and the staff always has had a number who are in college, often for their graduate studies.

Each guide goes through a course of training in the Center, lasting a couple of weeks, and then writes her own "spiel." This is edited, but it remains hers, and makes her seem more natural. At the same time she must be well enough informed to ad-lib answers to questions which may or may not have to do with the tour.

A guide is expected to know where sculptor Carl Milles was born (Uppsala) and maybe what his name was originally (Anderson), how many people attend the Music Hall every year (six million), what material was most used in building the Center (cinders by volume, sand by weight, although there is more than a quarter-million tons of structural steel, too). She is also expected to know what to do when, after she has informed the tour that there are fifty-seven thousand telephones in the Center, some brash young man says, "Never mind the fifty-seven thousand, what's your number?" (Smile sweetly and move on.)

Over the years the tours have recruited guides for many needs and special groups. There is a routine for the blind, who are as ardent tourists as anybody, conducted by a girl who can describe it all without using such words as "look" and "see." The deaf are escorted by a guide "speaking" an improvised sign language. With advance notice, the Center can produce a young woman proficient in French, German, Italian, or Spanish—she gets a premium of $5 a week.

Each girl averages five tours a day, seventeen visitors to the tour because the capacity of the elevators is eighteen. A minimum of five guides are on duty, as on weekdays in winter. Holidays and during the summer the troupe is augmented to as many as sixteen, still averaging five tours a day. On such occasions some tight scheduling is called for, since a fresh group is dispatched every few minutes, but usually the rush coincides with a Sunday or holiday when the working day traffic through the Center is at a minimum. No doubt it was on such a day that an Australian visitor, returning to her New York friends from a tour of Rockefeller Center, exclaimed: "You Americans are wonderful! Imagine all that building just for show!"

The Rainbow Room and Rainbow Grill are on the more sophisticated side of Rockefeller Center entertainment—more expensive too. On the sixty-fifth floor of the RCA Building, these command views which, by day or night, draw exclamations of wonder. They are the outgrowth of what started as a promotion scheme without any more specific goal than to attract people to the Center.

When the RCA Building opened in 1933, there were no tenants for the topmost floors. Yet by the economics of the skyscraper, a landlord ought to get more rent the higher the tenant goes. At this time the Center was finding it hard enough to find anyone to pay the lower scales. So it seemed a good idea to use the top of the building for some purpose that would draw attention to the project. An amusement expert was hired to make a survey and suggestions, but nothing came of it. Perhaps it was just as well. One of his proposals was a clock large enough to be visible from the street and striking the quarter hours. This was to be accompanied by a system of beams of colored light projected into the sky in a series of prearranged signals to announce events of public interest, such as "the President is on the air"—Roosevelt had just inaugurated his famous "fireside chats." Another suggestion was that the Center display an enormous illuminated map of New York.

After somewhat more than a year of idea mongering, the amusement expert departed, leaving behind one practical but not sensational plan to use the topmost floors for restaurants and private dining rooms. The restaurants, serving luncheons and perhaps supplemented by other rooms such as luncheon clubs, would be an attractive feature for tenants. As night spots with popular entertainers and music to augment the thrill of being in the city's highest dining room, they would advertise the Center.

Decorated in a style to match the extravagant hopes entertained for it, the first of these opened on October 3, 1934, with Lucienne Boyer, a star imported from France, and an orchestra which was one of the most popular of the day. The decorative feature was a color organ which played a complete range of colors on the domed ceiling and gave the place the name it never lost, the Rainbow Room. The second week the show was even better. Beatrice Lillie was engaged, and not only brought Noel Coward as a guest star, but sang for the first time on any stage one of her most delightful, memorable songs, "Baby Doesn't Know."

It was a great introduction for a new, glamorous night spot, but the rates these performers charged could keep the Rainbow Room in the red indefinitely. Miss Boyer took $4,000 a week, Miss Lillie, $2,375. Once they had made their big splash with the big names, the management, which in those days was John Roy, a former Boston drama editor and Hotchkiss School teacher, began looking around for first-class talent carrying a smaller price tag. A considerable number of performers who were on their way up played the Rainbow Room in the next few years at a tenth or less of Miss Boyer's fee. Marge and Gower Champion were among the first. Edgar Bergen and Charlie McCarthy appeared before they were one of radio's most popular features. Mary Martin was there in 1939 at $200 a week, and old—timers still remember her entrancing songs. Ray Noble made his first American appearance at the Rainbow Room; Paul Draper added to a budding reputation there, and so did Alec Templeton, the blind pianist.

Meantime, the other side of the sixty-fifth floor opened, first as the Patio and then as the Rainbow Grill. Its entertainment then was less ambitious; the really smash feature was a dance contest, usually a waltz, for the audience every night with a bottle of champagne going to the winner. Winthrop Rockefeller remembers *not* winning and also that he preferred the Rainbow Room. His younger brother David did win one—a polka—with the girl he later married, Margaret McGrath.

The war ended night life on top of the RCA Building. The blackout regulations were almost enough to do that by themselves; a Rainbow Room sealed off from the view lost some of its charm. So in December, 1942, the room was closed

after lunch. Then, in 1950, it was opened again for cocktails
and pretheater meals, four to nine o'clock, while the Rainbow Grille, no longer the poor little sister, began offering
more typical night club entertainment. In 1964 both were
leased to the Brody Corporation.

New Yorkers pursuing pleasure can descend from the sixty-
fifth floor to the Lower Plaza across from the RCA Building.
Orphaned by the long delay in the Sixth Avenue subway, this
attractive rectangle failed as a passage bringing pedestrians
from the promenade into the shops that originally lined it.
After a couple of years of hesitation and debate, the shops
were replaced by a couple of restaurants, and the Lower
Plaza was no longer even a passage into the concourse. What
to do with it?

As a sunken garden, it was a pleasant eyecatcher, but that
was all. At last, in December, 1936, someone suggested flood-
ing it for ice skating. A band of enthusiasts patronized it so
ardently that in 1939 a permanent freezing system, circulat-
ing brine that can keep ice at just the right consistency for
skaters, was installed. The pond has been at least as attractive
to spectators as to performers. Lots of people, it is plain on
any winter's day that is not too stormy, love to stand above
and look down on novices, Olympic skating stars, talented
professionals, and run-of-the-mill skaters. A measure of the
skating rink's popularity is that one year the Center tried
roller skating after the ice was gone, but that was not so
successful.

The Center was a little slow in recognizing its unusual
open spaces for what they really are. It had been so long since
the city had anything like it that people were slow to realize
its potential. Its character developed gradually, and all of a
sudden everybody said why, of course, it is New York's village
green.

It started really in May, 1934, while the sunken garden still was supposed to be a link to the concourse, with a concert by Sousa's Band which, although the master had been dead a couple of years, was the most famous aggregation of brass in America. In November, a huge board to register election returns was set up. Gradually, promoters of causes, anniversaries, memorials, and a host of civic and commercial enterprises discovered that Rockefeller Center, with its gardens and fountains and roofs and most importantly the two hundred thousand people who are there on business every day was an admirable place to stage any sort of event which in simpler days would have been held on a village green.

What is wanted, by the promoters anyway, is a large, open space with curious people going by, many of them with nothing much to do. While the people are there in almost any downtown New York area, so that a crowd will collect for anything or nothing, the number of open spaces with an attractive background is small.

Fortunately for the Center's reputation and the peace of its tenants, this area is still private property, and the management can turn down those applicants it considers too noisy, too blatantly commercial, in bad taste, or otherwise unsuitable. Rejections and permissions are a function of the Public Relations Department, which exercises with tact the unpopular role of arbiter. Diplomacy is required to explain, for example, to an aspiring entrepreneur whose feelings one does not wish to offend that his bevy of scantily clad bathing beauties does not quite meet Rockefeller Center's village green standards.

There remain plenty of events that do meet the standards. Some of them are annuals, repeated pretty much in the same form year after year. Armed Forces Week, National Maritime Day, the rally for launching the United Hospital Fund campaign, the book collection of the American Merchant Marine which fills a full-sized lifeboat set up there for the purpose, a rally of vintage car enthusiasts—these are samples of the things that come to the village green, usually with music, sometimes with entertainment, almost always with speeches.

An even larger roster of one-shot events staged at Rockefeller Center could be compiled. The place has seen War Loan Drives and bunny shows with hundreds of live rabbits at Easter, a Holland bulb festival and bicentenary ceremonies for Lafayette, celebrations of the Liberation of Paris and the coronation of Queen Elizabeth, the Golden Jubilee of the electric light, the revival of the Sidewalk Superintendents Club—one could go on for pages.

All of these events and attractions, and just the attraction of the place itself, bring to the Center a lot of people who do not know where they are going or how they got here in the first place. They became so numerous that at last, partly in self-defense, the Center organized an information service to tell about the rest of New York. It turns out that some visitors know how to get to Rockefeller Center but not to any other spot.

Since 1962, the service in the RCA Building's main lobby has been maintained regularly by uniformed receptionists who can tell the puzzled stranger how to get back to his hotel or what hotel might have a room, what to see and how to get to it, how to make phone calls, where to shop, and how much to tip. Shortly after this was opened, a study of the first twenty-seven thousand people served showed that 11 percent were foreign visitors. Now answers to questions can be made on the spot in Spanish, French, German, Italian, Portuguese, Greek, Finnish, Hungarian, Dutch, Swedish, Danish, and Norwegian. For Polish, Hebrew, Russian, Slovak, Turkish, Armenian, Ukranian and Maltese, the receptionist can call in a volunteer from among the employees.

If you have to get lost in New York, therefore, Rockefeller Center is a good place for it. The information girls have located a French visitor's luncheon partner at a nearby hotel by patient telephoning although the poor fellow had not the faintest notion of its name or what part of the city it might be in. A bewildered Jamaican medical student was placed in touch with the proper hospital authorities to consult on his specialty. A distraught suitor, or maybe husband, was advised where he could buy Hungarian candy.

During the 1964–65 New York World's Fair, this service was supplemented by an outdoor information booth in the Atlas Court on Fifth Avenue. It handled a thousand inquiries a day, about as many as the fair got concerning Rockefeller Center.

If this seems to be rather an innovation for a village green, the Christmas tree brings the Center back into the traditional concept, but on a grander-than-village scale. Actually, there is never another Christmas tree in the whole world like this one. A children's book has been written about it, *The Most Beautiful Tree in the World.* The tree is seen by millions on television and thousands come to the city for no other purpose. The size is just one imposing feature; one year it was a spruce ninety feet tall; the smallest was a fifty-foot pine.

The Christmas tree idea started small, which alone makes it unusual for Rockefeller Center. On the other hand, it started early. It was set up off Fifth Avenue late in December, 1931, by workmen who were excavating for the British Empire Building and La Maison Francaise. It was the standard apartment house tree, maybe twenty-five feet tall. That year the bulldozers worked right up to dark on Christmas Eve—an extra hour or two of pay was important—and before the men went home they got their money in front of the tree.

One year it was the turn of the men of steel. The skeleton of a new Time & Life Building was rising, and to the top the

Rockefeller Center's first Christmas tree. It was erected by workmen who had just completed demolition and were beginning excavations for the first two buildings. The photograph shows them collecting their pay on Christmas Eve, 1931.

workers hoisted another tree, a bigger one and all lit up. People with good eyesight could see it from the street and were cheered.

In 1933 management took over. Ever since, the Christmas tree has been erected in Rockefeller Plaza and decorated by the Center. Its arrival has been big news for more than thirty years, and the throwing of the switch to light it on the first Thursday in December is considered the official opening of the Christmas season in New York. The decorations quickly became so elaborate and so ingenious that in order to top it

The 1958 Christmas display. The view is from Fifth Avenue west across the Channel Gardens and the Prometheus statue to the Christmas tree in Rockefeller Plaza.

or even match it, the Center has been known to get to work on December 26 to plan the tree for next year. For the first twenty-four years, the designs were created by Robert Carson, whose firm, Carson & Lundin, were Rockefeller Center's resident architects. Since then, they have been the work of the Center's Architectural and Display Division.

Nearly every New Yorker has his favorite among the themes. A lot of votes would go to the 1958 version of the line from C. F. Alexander's hymn, "All things bright and beautiful, all creatures great and small." Valerie Clarebout, an English sculptor, that year modeled fifty-four creatures of the forest in brass and aluminum wire. They ranged through the Channel Gardens—lordly deer with lights twinkling on their majestic golden antlers, field mice and birds, rabbits and foxes. Or some would go back to 1951 when from Fifth Avenue to the skating pond twin rows of twelve simulated fountains each seemed to splash and bubble in a pale, blue light while an effect of cascades and shimmering pools was achieved by the use of other lights beamed through revolving disks. And, of course, a great many people think every year is best.

The trees themselves are the object of long and careful search. In early summer, the Center's scouts are out looking for the perfect evergreen. Many who see the result think they must have been tramping the north woods. But no forest specimen ever is so tall, straight, and symmetrical, with such good healthy foliage on every side. Only trees grown in isolation fill the Rockefeller Center requirements. Once found, their owners are not usually reluctant to part with them. A tree of this size and quality is old, sixty-five years or more, which is a ripe age for an evergreen in this part of the world. A big blow may topple it any year.

Most of them have come from within one hundred miles of New York, which is well because a transportation problem is involved. However, the states of New Hampshire, Vermont, Massachusetts, and Maine have presented perfect specimens to the Center for the people of New York. The two tallest, ninety and eighty-five feet, came from the estates of Carll Tucker and Hollingsworth Wood in Mount Kisco, a New York City suburb.

Such a giant calls for a crew of twenty men and some heavy machinery to get it to Rockefeller Center. The branches are bound tight against the trunk, just like any Christmas tree you see stacked outside a florist's shop, only a winch is needed to do it. As the trunk is sawed through, a twenty-ton crane and two tractors ease it onto a fifty-foot log trailer for the trip to Manhattan. A vast amount of telephoning, conferring, and charting clears the route to the city so there will not be too many traffic jams and also to be sure the tree will pass safely under overpasses and viaducts.

The decorations will have been custom made for it, mostly in Rockefeller Center's own facilities, because the ready-made items are almost invariably too small and too fragile. Everything on this tree has to withstand a month or more exposed to the wind, soot, rain, sleet, and snow of a New York winter. Metals that will not corrode, tinsel that will keep its glitter in spite of dust and soot, and garlands that a heavy wind cannot tear apart are not easy to come by and not really easy to make. A lot of them get tested during the year, mostly on the Center's rooftops and terraces. Tenants looking out of their windows in August and seeing a linden tree on the eleventh floor roof garden dripping aluminum icicles know that Christmas is in the planning.

Waterproofing all the delicate-looking decorations is per-haps the toughest job. Once, in fact, it did not come off, because the winter conditions are not always duplicated in summer. The design called for 324 gold and white candles in the Channel Gardens, and they looked very fine. But the waterproofing was imperfect, and in the first heavy rain, the horrified designers saw their candles almost literally melting away. The men in the shops worked all that night, and by the time holiday visitors arrived the next day 324 new candles were flickering in their neat rows, but it had been a near catastrophe.

For twenty years the tree lighting, which is now done with considerable ceremony, was featured by a pleasant village green touch which has been lost, the carol singing of an old-fashioned folk chorus. It was composed of men and women who worked in Rockefeller Center, liked to sing, and had voices which their highly discriminating director, John R. Jones, would pass. Known as the Rockefeller Center Choristers, these enthusiastic amateurs developed in the great tradition of village or church or college choral groups, and they needed all their zeal. An icy gale blew snow flurries across the plaza to greet their 1939 Christmas inaugural. Their director remembers them "hanging onto robes and caps and music, and by sheer grit singing 'And the Glory of the Lord' from Handel's 'Messiah' through chattering teeth, while noses grew red and faces blue."

The Choristers went on, performing at a great variety of events on their village green through the years, until Jones retired in 1959. They were discontinued after that; their role now is taken by other groups, some amateur, some professional.

In the general entertainment picture of Rockefeller Center, some of the greatest variety and greatest change has been in the museums and exhibitions which have been housed here. Exhibitions of a temporary nature are to be expected in any buildings visited by so many people and with such obvious facilities for displaying anything from postage stamps to computers. But that a commercial development should have attracted so many long-lived museums is a little surprising.

Not that most of them are as permanent fixtures as NBC or Time & Life or Standard Oil. But they do remain at Rockefeller Center for years on end, some of them.

The Museum of Modern Art had its quarters in galleries under what is now the General Dynamics Building for a couple of years in the late 1930's, before it moved to its permanent home on West Fifty-third Street. When that happened Wallace Harrison and Nelson Rockefeller, both of whom had a more than mild interest in the museum, cherished a dream of continuing Rockefeller Plaza right through from Fifty-first Street to Fifty-third Street, and achieving a sort of museum-gallery complex next to the commercial and entertainment development. At Nelson's request, Harrison even drew up some designs, made some sketches, but there it stopped.

Even earlier, as a device for attracting people into the shopping areas, a Museum of Science and Industry was operated until 1949. It displayed a long series of electrical, mechanical, chemical, and physical wonders, concluding with one on postwar German industry. At various times there have been "permanent" exhibitions of decorative arts and crafts, a United States Rubber Exhibition Hall, and an American Cyanamid Exhibit, all lasting for years. Of the four in existence when this book was written, the Money Museum is the dean.

But the major entertainment that draws audiences to Rockefeller Center is and always has been motion pictures. More than thirty years after its inauspicious opening, the Radio City Music Hall remains the premier motion picture house of the nation and the only one still featuring a majestic stage show. Many of these are still produced by the temperamental and industrious Leonidoff in his own inimitable style, which runs to a dozen grand pianos on stage for one number and three Roman chariots with live horses for another. Throughout the auditorium and the lobbies the world's biggest theater still glitters and shines just as it did when it was new, and New York is a lot fonder of it now. When it closed for five days early in 1965 for a thorough cleaning, the newspapers ran long, cooing stories about it as if it had been the city's new baby getting its first bath.

The place still draws more than six million patrons a year and sold a ticket to its two hundred millioneth customer some time ago. For some of its holiday shows, it still finds ten thousand people standing in line of a morning and presenting a pedestrian problem as the queue winds around the block and the foresighted, patient standers munch their sandwiches. Russell V. Downing, Eyssell's successor here, who had been with the Music Hall since he was brought in as corporate treasurer to grapple with its financial woes during the first year, says long lines in the morning are not always signs of a smash hit. Sometimes a picture which the kids love will not quite fill the house at night.

Indeed, the problem of finding pictures for the Music Hall's policy—appealing to the whole family—gets more difficult every year. This is a policy professed by a good many showmen, but few of them in the theater business are as bound to it by both necessity—those 6,200 seats—and inclination, as is the screening committee of six men and a woman who choose what the Music Hall will show. They only need about ten features a year these days as against the forty-seven of the first year, but the ten are no easier to book. In the first place, fewer pictures are being made than in the days before television. Secondly, the changing styles in moviemaking limit the choice for this particular theater still further, for an increasing number of the best features are extremely long, much too long for the Music Hall's policy, which calls for the stage show at each performance. But the third and more serious obstacle is the producers' notion of the ingredients which make up what a considerable segment of the industry calls an "adult" film. The trend, some of the spokesmen have explained, is toward "adult" themes and situations because that is what modern audiences demand. However, it would seem in the peculiar jargon of Hollywood it is supposed that, just as "infant" means an individual in a state of infancy, so "adult" means an individual in a state of adultery. While Downing, now retired, might not put it just that way, he had a hard time booking movies that were up to the Music Hall's production standards and to which, furthermore, a man would be willing to take his wife, daughter, and mother.

The business of selecting a film for the Music Hall is quite an enterprise, even without this complication. Very often it begins with the script and before casting. A few sent to him by producers usually can be seen on Downing's desk in what used to be part of Roxy's apartment in the Music Hall. The producers not only want to submit it for a possible feature in his house, but they want the benefit of his experience in judging the story and suggesting the leads, for he has the reputation of being uncannily right when he plumps all out for a picture as one the public will consider a hit. Any of the selections, especially the Christmas or Easter film, may be booked from the rough, uncut, unscored version six months before the release date.

The whole operation may be summed up as a race. The Music Hall management has to run very hard to stay in the same place. Nothing demonstrates this so well as the new screen, projection equipment, and light console, all of which have to be kept up to the last minute. The console has 4,305 switches and can be preset, along with the curtain, in endless combinations, operated finally by pulling one master switch. The four projectors run about 25 million feet of film a year, throwing the image 190 feet to the screen.

The Music Hall has slightly more than 25,000 light bulbs, the smallest being 2 watts and the largest, 5,000. It consumes about the same amount of electricity as a city of 10,000 people even though its 6,200 patrons sit in the dark.

Nothing demonstrates the continuing popularity of the Music Hall as well as the forty-six young women known as the Rockettes. It is so good, or bad, that wherever Downing travels about in the world as President of the Music Hall Corporation, people to whom he is so introduced say, "Ah, yes, the Rockettes." Maybe the secret of their phenomenal popularity everywhere is that as a troupe of precision dancers they never get a day older.

They are still trained by the man who devised the first routine. Markert in his sixties does not hoof it with the same

The Rockettes, the 36 of them who are on stage at any one time.

abandon he did when he was fifty, but he still maintains the standard of precision he set from the very beginning. There are always forty-six members of the troupe, although only thirty-six are on stage at one time; the other ten are enjoying their one week off out of four, which sounds generous until you realize they work a very long day seven days a week. They have not been there forever, as they seem; they average about five years on the line. The dropouts are usually due to marriage and child-bearing, not age, for they are nearly always in their early twenties still. As for their qualifications, Markert makes them sound simple: "About the only thing Rockettes must have in common is long legs and the knack of memorizing a complicated routine, the way an actor memorizes lines."

From the audience, one would think they also have to be the same height but, in fact, this may vary as much as three inches. The gradation in the line is too slight to notice. And, of course, they are young; most are about seventeen when they start and few are more than twenty.

The mechanical perfection is such that years of dancing together would seem mandatory. Yet new girls fit in very quickly. Markert says it takes only about twenty hours of drill for the Rockettes to master a new routine; that's where the ability to memorize is needed.

What happens to a Rockette when she leaves? Is it a road to stardom? The answer to the first question is often marriage, and to the second, is usually no. Only a few spinsters, only a few name dancers have turned up among the hundreds of alumnae—Adele Jergens, Joan Vohs, Lucille Bremer, and Vera-Ellen are perhaps the best known. Most Rockettes do not become stars because subordinating personality and individuality deliberately, as their routines demand, is hardly the training for a solo performer.

Smaller stages in the outside world are more likely to take on young people from the Music Hall's singers and from the ballet of thirty-two dancers. Metropolitan Opera stars Jan Peerce, Robert Weede, Leonard Warren, and Robert Merrill gained reputations at the Music Hall; so did ballerinas Norah Kaye and Melissa Hayden.

One other thing besides husbands and babies happens to most ex-Rockettes. They organize. They have an active Alumnae Association in which two of the dancers from the old Roxy played leading founder roles, Mrs. B. Allen Magee and Mrs. Harry Mayer, known then and now as "Dinky." They have been joined by about three hundred of their successors and devote themselves to raising funds for charity: a typical Rockette Alumnae dinner dance was for the benefit of the National Association for the Help of Retarded Children.

All in all, the steady success of the Music Hall has been undimmed, which makes all the more mysterious the fading of its contemporary, the Center Theater. By 1950 the popularity of ice shows no longer warranted the extended runs needed to prosper in this house, but the rapid growth of television gave it a breather. NBC leased it as a studio-playhouse, and for a time its large auditorium and excellent backstage facilities were invaluable. It was television's biggest theater, and some of its audiences expected to be on the air indefinitely. Within three years, the same growth that brought television to the Center Theater took it out again. The stage and facilities were no longer suitable; the huge audiences were no longer desired. NBC gave up its lease in 1953, and the house went dark, with no takers in sight. As a factor in the world of entertainment, it could hardly be called a success; its room was more desirable than its still elegant presence. The United States Rubber Company was seeking expansion, and the site of the doomed hall of pleasure was perfect for that. By the end of 1954 the last vestige of it had vanished in a complex pattern of girders wrapping themselves around the United States Rubber Building.

In retrospect, it still seems strange and wonderful that this has not been the fate of more of the Rockefeller Center entertainment features. After all, it is odd that fun and games should be so large a part of an urban center whose serious purpose is to house profitably and well the offices of a thousand big and little serious businesses. But, obviously, the Center does not live by work alone.

13

The Road to a Man's Heart

Strangers seeing New York's commercial districts at the noon hour may be forgiven if they suppose that the major industry in this city is lunch. Everybody, but just everybody, seems single-mindedly bent on getting food and drink, and that is not all. That this is the busiest hour the telephone company well knows because many persons have to call for a reservation, an appointment, an order, or to change one of these. Perhaps the stranger will be even more astonished to discover that the people he meets at this time think theirs is quite the normal procedure of all civilized business men and women in pursuit of a midday meal.

Since the architects who designed Rockefeller Center considered that their primary purpose was to fit the buildings to the activities, needs, and comfort of the workers in them, this daily phenomenon had to be taken into account. To the management of the completed structures, it is an even more serious problem. While no one ever supposed that it would be either possible or desirable to feed the Center's entire population on the premises, the necessity for restaurants that could accommodate a considerable number was recognized. Some New Yorkers, to be sure, regard going out to lunch as a must, but others think there is something efficient or cozy or convenient about not leaving their own buildings.

In the early 1930's, however, office workers, even many at the executive level, were literally pulling in their belts. A good, filling if not nourishing 25-cent lunch was as much as a great many of them ever contemplated. Others had given up lunch altogether as a needless extravagance. So there was no very noticeable public clamor for more eating places, nor did examination of the right-hand side of typical menus around town encourage anyone to commit himself to the sort of rents Rockefeller Center had to have. In fact, when the RCA and RKO Buildings were opened, it has been recorded, the operators of restaurants had to be "induced" to come in and serve food.

The most open to persuasion, it appears, was the Union News Company, which feeds people as well as supplying them with current reading matter. It received as a reward for its courage the first refusal of any new restaurants which might be contemplated in any of the Center buildings. Under this arrangement the Union News at one time actually did operate all the eating places in the development, including the Rainbow Room and Grill after 1942.

Fortunately, eating proved to be one of the first activities the public resumed after the worst of the Depression, and Rockefeller Center shared in the benefit. More and more eating places were opened as the number of buildings increased until at last there were twenty-seven, including two big private luncheon clubs. A half dozen of them would be in any comprehensive roster of New York's better restaurants, three or four on most tourist lists of interesting places to dine. But in the middle of the day they are strictly business, whether sandwich counter, cafeteria, coffee shop, or luxury dining room.

As in most of the city, it is possible also to drink your lunch, but that was not originally the intention. Designed, begun, and its first seven buildings completed during the era of national Prohibition, the center was suspected at one time of becoming a desert in the oasis of repeal. There was some question that even if the law permitted spirituous and malt beverages, the mainstay of certain classes of establishments operated for man's refreshment, they would not be allowed here. However, two weeks after Roosevelt's inauguration in 1933 and with the end of Prohibition almost in sight, the directors of Rockefeller Center adopted this policy:

In the event that the sale of liquor is permitted by law, Rockefeller Center, Inc., will prohibit the sale of liquor in saloons but will permit such sale in legitimate restaurants and clubs under rigid regulations to be established by Rockefeller Center, as landlord, violation of such regulations to call for a cancellation of the lease.

Fortunately for the comfort and convenience of patrons and the success of the many spots in the Center where a man can buy a drink, no one apparently ever bothered to look up the word "saloon" in the dictionary. There you have to get to the fourth definition before you find anything at all relevant, and then it turns out to mean a place where drinks are sold. The directors obviously were harking back to the bad old days before the Eighteenth Amendment when the "saloon evil" was the favorite topic of Prohibitionists, and they seem to have known only the places with swinging doors, long bars, and ragged, tearful children outside. Anyway, the Center developed just like any other area in town except that none of the shops sell liquor by the bottle, which most of the old pre-Prohibition saloons did not sell either.

The development was such, in fact, that it has been suggested more business is transacted over the luncheon tables in Rockefeller Center than across its desks. This doubtful statistic is perhaps inspired by the fact that there are more eating places than buildings. But they are not all the same type of eating places, nor under the same management, as in the beginning.

One reason why the number of operators has increased is that the Union News Company's first refusal agreement expired in 1948, and that phase of it was not renewed. The reason for the changes in the type of restaurants themselves is more complex and has to do with the economics of the luncheon business in New York.

The life and death of a restaurant which was started in La Maison Francaise is an excellent case history for the study of that business, but one doubts that it throws much light on academic economics. At the outset, it seemed obvious that a building with this name ought to have a first-class French restaurant. The right man for the right place was available as its chef, guiding spirit, and lessee. He was Henri Charpentier, a famous French cook whose reputation and personality seemed to guarantee success. He gave just the proper Gallic gourmet touch to his dining room, but unfortunately his business acumen was not the equal of his culinary skill. He served superb meals, but had not gauged their cost properly, and before long he stopped paying his rent. The Center reluctantly evicted him and turned the place over to Union News.

As the Café Louis XIV it was successful enough for some time but began to show signs of wear in the 1950's just at a time when the competition was becoming keener and expenses larger. Facing on Forty-ninth Street, the Louis XIV took up space and required the sort of staff and maintenance which demanded a gross income of about a million dollars a year to be profitable. It was not doing much better than a third of that. In an effort to build it up again, Union News poured a good deal of money into it at the end of the 1950's with a substantial redecorating job, including a new bar. But it seems people do not especially yearn for a French restaurant in La Maison Francaise. Anyway, the Café Louis XIV, although it doubled its business, could not reach its goal and closed.

Meanwhile, a block away on Forty-eighth street in the United States Rubber Company Addition, the Forum of the Twelve Caesars was exceeding expectations in the same years. This was not only a new location for a restaurant, requiring the building of kitchens and installation of all the complicated equipment for service and bar, but it was not regarded by many as a very desirable location. Although the Rockefeller Center address was fine, the entrance faced a row of discount merchants and old stores or offices on the other side of the street.

However, the operators, Restaurant Associates, a firm with several high-priced eating establishments in several big office buildings around town, had an idea and a menu which caught on famously. The customer was (and is) invited to sample dishes such as made the feasts of the Roman Empire a sybaritic legend. Some of them—a peacock done more or less as Augustus may have had it, for example—have to be ordered three days ahead of time and cost in the neighborhood of two hundred dollars. But such items as Roman leeks, Apician style, or wild boar you can get almost any time. People also like the portraits of the dozen emperors for whom the place is named presiding over their feasts. So the Forum of the Twelve Caesars surpassed the minimum rental guarantee the very first month it was open, although it had only twenty days of the month left, and within six months was grossing about twice what it had calculated as necessary to show a profit.

It was hardly surprising that shortly thereafter this same company was selected to operate the new and largest restaurant in Rockefeller Center, designed to seat four hundred guests on the street floor of the new Time & Life Building. Since a specialty had worked so well on one side of the Avenue of the Americas, a similar formula was adopted on the other. Perhaps because of the avenue's name, it was decided to borrow some culinary ideas from Mexico and South America and give the dining room itself a Spanish name, La Fonda del Sol or Inn of the Sun. One visual attraction for patrons is to watch beef roasting over thirty feet of open fires against one wall. In the same building a penthouse shelters a restaurant called the Tower Suite and a luncheon club called the Hemisphere. Forty-eight stories high, it has a view rivaling that of the Rainbow Room, and the seating was arranged so that a much larger proportion of the tables get the benefit of it.

The Rainbow Room's own luncheon club is the oldest in the Center, having opened in 1934, even earlier than the night club there. It has been one of the attractive features of tenancy as the roster of 1,100 members indicates. It has had a more than usually distinguished roster of governors, the board being drawn largely from top officers of large companies with headquarters in one of the buildings.

The Center's two oldest continuously successful eating places in the upper price brackets were afterthoughts. When it turned out that the Lower Plaza did not bring pedestrians streaming into the concourse shops and the shops at this point had to be abandoned, their space was turned into two restaurants opening onto the plaza, a Café Francaise in La Maison Francaise and an English Grill in the British Empire

Building. The attraction of the skaters in winter and of the colors of the Prometheus fountain in summer apparently never dims. In 1964, outdoor dancing in summer was revived in the Lower Plaza, so both restaurants added supper menus to their repertoire.

All these are the upper crust of the Center's pie. The vast majority of the people content themselves with less luxurious, less leisurely, and less expensive lunches. So there are eighteen places in Rockefeller Center that cater to the more typical New Yorkers. The concern of the management in maintaining the variety is that only so can the prosperity of most of them be assured. The customary lease for restaurant space, as for all the shops, is a minimum rent supplemented by a percentage of the business' take. It is as important to the Center as to the business that this be more than just enough to keep going. The landlord becomes in effect a partner and prospers only if the tenant does.

That is why, when new space for a popular eating place is opened in Rockefeller Center, the management solicits both bids for rent and ideas for the type of establishment to be operated. The one that offers the best promise of heavy patronage is accepted. Thus, when it came time to consider how average lunchers were to be accommodated in the Time & Life Building, the Union News Company's proposal won out. The reason? Its "imaginative presentation featuring a Sandwich Palace" suggested a rather unusual and therefore perhaps profitable future for that American luncheon specialty. Underneath this particular area, which is on the concourse, Union News was even permitted to install its own bakery.

While traditionally the urban office building is deserted at night except for cleaners and an occasional late clerical worker or executive, a good many of the Rockefeller Center restaurants do a thriving dinner business. They are located close enough to the bulk of New York's night life, especially the theaters and night clubs, that half of them remain open after the offices close. Some of the more elegant ones even do better from the evening trade than from the more frenzied midday throngs.

14

"The Last Rivet"

On November 1, 1939, a little knot of distinguished citizens watched John D. Rockefeller, Jr., drive a rivet. It was a reasonably historic occasion, not just gratifying the whim of a man who liked to build, which his son Nelson says was one of his suppressed desires. That rivet was supposed to be the last of some ten million which completed the frame of the fourteenth and final building of Rockefeller Center, to be named for the United States Rubber Company.

As he held the riveting machine and prepared to deliver a little speech expressive of his beliefs in this sort of enterprise, Mr. Junior could have been permitted a sense of triumph. But if he felt it, he did not show it. Nor was he tempted by it to heed the request which Mayor Fiorello La Guardia had just made. His Honor had told the assembled guests and spectators that the whole city was proud of the Center as an

John D. Rockefeller, Jr. driving "the last rivet" into the frame of the United States Rubber Building, the fourteenth and supposedly final structure of the project, on Nov. 1, 1939. Many millions more have been driven since then in the newer buildings.

outstanding monument, and a useful one.

"It is comfortable in these times to have one of these taxpayers around—comforting and rather helpful," the Little Flower went on. "May I ask, Mr. Rockefeller, will you please look around and see if you can put a few more Centers around the city?"

No, he was not tempted to do that. In an atmosphere of great good will, which is typical of such ceremonies, he was content to let well enough alone. The project had proved itself; the years of deficits were ending; the next twelve months would see the turning point in the profit and loss ledger. After that the center would not only make money—it began paying federal income taxes for the year 1944 and never stopped—it would in time be able to repay some of the investment. The founder would have no more sleepless nights on this score nor have to sell stocks at sacrifice prices to pay the bills.

He performed efficiently his star role of rivet driver and sat back, a quiet observer of the ceremonies. He seemed much more restrained in his enthusiasm than Nelson, who as president of the Center sat beaming beside His Honor on the platform. Rockefeller was flanked by his landlord, President Butler of Columbia, and by his principal tenant, David Sarnoff, president of RCA. In the audience were many of the architects, engineers, builders, lawyers, businessmen, and assorted advisers who had staffed the project.

One would have been surprised to hear anything but nice things on such an occasion. Nevertheless, one of the tributes was a little unusual. It came from the head of the Building and Construction Trades Council, Thomas A. Murray, and expressed the gratitude of the many thousands who had been employed for so long "at a time when, frankly, our members very badly needed work." Murray went on to speak with obvious satsifaction of the absence of strikes throughout the job, of the fact that there had been "no dispute which was not readily adjusted over the conference table."

It could have been a time for retrospect. When La Guardia mentioned the Center's role as taxpayer, the mayor was thinking no doubt of the $2,551,909 which would be paid to the city in real estate levies alone for the current year, three times the amount of 1930. The land had been assessed at $31,253,000 then and at only $33,066,000 in 1939, but the buildings went from zero to $53,439,400 in the same period. (The whole of Rockefeller Center was assessed at $245,000,-000 at the time this book was written and pays more than $11,000,000 in real estate taxes.)

One might look back at the difficulty the Center had in attracting tenants to the new buildings six years before. The lures Nelson Rockefeller had dangled so skillfully then were no longer necessary at the end of 1939. Nearly 100 percent occupancy was already guaranteed for the United States Rubber Company Building when it should be ready to receive tenants in five months, and the rest of the Center was virtually fully rented.

Perhaps a man with a well-organized mind might wish to review the welter of groups, committees, and corporations that had been formed, revised, and dissolved, most of them, to get the job done. Probably no one could even count the committees, but there had been no fewer than seventeen corporations in addition to the Metropolitan Square Corporation and Rockefeller Center, Inc., each performing some function of art, realty, law, finance, service, or operations.

But perhaps it was also a time for anticipation. Was the future of Rockefeller Center merely the maintenance of what had been done? Apparently, the founder supposed that this would be so, perhaps he hoped it would be, too. To preserve the fourteen buildings and all the outdoor spaces and to keep them up-to-date and in tune with the lastest equipment and processes, would be a task of sufficient magnitude for anyone. However, the men gathered to watch Rockefeller operate a riveting machine were mostly well aware that hardly anything of man's creation is static.

At that particular moment, all mankind was poised for one of the greatest eras of change in human history. Not very prominent in the news of the day was what some commentators were beginning to call the "Sitzkrieg." It had succeeded the "Blitzkrieg" launched by Nazi Germany against Poland only two months earlier. In less than three weeks, what was supposed to be one of the strongest armies in Europe except for those of the big powers had been crushed. Already, however, the wonder of it—and the lesson, too—was fading as German armies confronted the French ensconced confortably in their Maginot Line which was supposed to make their country impregnable. Communiques and reports of casualties were hardly as exciting as the carnage on American highways. But reflective men were wondering what the real effects of this conflict, now in its "phony war" stage, were going to be; the only thing one could be sure of was that they would be profound.

On Rockefeller Center in the next years one obvious effect was to confirm the impression that Mr. Junior's last rivet really was the last. Materials and labor for commercial construction unrelated to war soon became extremely scarce. People had other interests, too. Within a year of the rivet ceremony, Rockefeller Center's president was in Washington as the head of a new government agency devoted to our relations with the Latin American republics. Some of his Center aides, notably Harrison and Borella, followed him, while the Army, Navy, Air Force, and assorted war jobs claimed many others.

In some ways those years are almost a hiatus in the story of this piece of real estate. Management grappled with shortages of personnel and supplies, and new people were being trained constantly for routine jobs. It was impossible to have always on hand a comfortably ample supply of so simple a commodity as soap. Watchmen had to worry about being sure tenants and the Center staff observed the blackout regulations. An extensive apparatus of volunteers to serve in any enemy bombing emergency was created and drilled, manned by workers in many of the offices as well as by employees of the Center but, fortunately, they never had to meet an emergency.

The entry of the United States into the war was marked by the seizure of premises occupied by German, Italian, and Japanese tenants. The seizure was done by the Army and FBI mostly, and with an unobtrusiveness that was disappointing to some of the more excitable tenants. Within a few months, the government had removed all traces of the alien occupants, and there was no dearth of applicants for the vacant space.

Some of the hush-hush operations of the British were conducted from here. One former intelligence officer remembers owing his life—he is pretty sure he would not otherwise have survived his assignment—to getting out unseen through the incredible mazes of the Center's subbasement. Another sign of the times was the temporary obliteration of the name of the Palazzo d'Italia, while the coat of arms of the House of Savoy, Kings of Italy, was boarded over. The RCA Building was, however, embellished by one of the larger air raid warning sirens.

This hardly added up to much excitement when spread over five years. For the most part, the routine of the Center remained as undisturbed as any place in the city. But the period did see one interesting point of law and landlord-tenant relationship settled, a point with wider implications than just this one development. It was also part of what has been a varied struggle by Rockefeller Center to protect its fair name from outside exploitation. This particular one lasted for more than five years, and in the course of it some safeguards were erected for a lot of other good names.

It all began in March, 1935, when even small offices were not so easy to rent. One of the smallest in what still was known as the RKO Building was leased by Isidore Mitchell, a dealer in second-hand jewelry and other merchandize. He was not expected to be what Nelson Rockefeller calls a blue-chip tenant, but the Center's renting department had no idea how far from blue they would find him.

A clause in his lease provided that he might assign it to a corporation he would form later. The day after he had signed, he informed the Center that he was assigning his lease to a company he had just organized under the name of the Rockefeller Purchasing Corporation.

If the Center's management had been a little less dignified, their reaction to this news could only have been described as hitting the ceiling. The idea of a second-hand trade of the sort Mitchell obviously contemplated being carried on in Rockefeller Center under the Rockefeller name was intolerable.

The renting department firmly told Mitchell that the assignment of his lease could not and would not be countenanced. He responded with the insistence that it was not within the landlord's province to approve or disapprove the name of his company; he had a right to assign the lease to it, and he brought suit to enforce that right. The center took up the challenge and argued that he had to choose some other name than Rockefeller.

In the course of the litigation Mitchell was quite frank to admit that he planned a very large advertising campaign to exploit the Rockefeller aspect of his Purchasing Corporation, and he expected to make his fortune just from using that name and his new address. He also said that no one connected with his corporation really was entitled to be called Rockefeller, but he could correct that if the courts felt it would strengthen his case. He knew a dog wagon cook in Rochester named Dan Rockefeller, and Mitchell was quite prepared to make him an officer in the Rockefeller Purchasing Corporation.

The Center, of course, maintained that this would be an outrageous, illegal, immoral, and altogether inadmissible exploitation of a respected name. But in law it was not so clear that Mitchell's claim, ethically questionable as it might be, would not stand. The case provided the impetus for a campaign to correct the law, and the courts were not even halfway through deciding the issue in 1937 when the legislature of New York added a new crime to the penal code. That year it became a misdemeanor to adopt and use any name with intent to deceive or mislead the public. The courts were authorized to enjoin such conduct, and under the new law people have been prevented from exploiting their own real names when the effect would constitute fraud.

But criminal laws of this kind may not be made retroactive; legislatures do not have the power in this country to say anything may be adjudged a crime after the fact. So Mitchell's case remained in the courts. It went through eleven trials altogether, culminating in the Court of Appeals, the state's highest tribunal, before Mitchell was defeated at last in 1940.

That was the year, too, for the opening of the Sixth Avenue subway—the old elevated train had run its last car two years earlier. It was a boon to the tenants who faced that way and added enormously to the accessibility of Rockefeller Center. Indeed, it was such an improvement that the city promptly assessed all the property owners for the extra light and air they gained from the elevated's removal. The Center's share was $60,565.01, and while it would not have sold these rights for a lot more than that, it and the other tenants protested that the sum was too high. They won, and the bills were cut in half. The settlement came just before the formal change of the name from Sixth Avenue to Avenue of the Americas, which cost nothing.

By this time the war was over, and in the rejoicing at the return of peace, it was still possible to suppose that Rockefeller Center was complete. But difficult as it is to start something like this, it is harder still to apply the brakes. Anyone with vision, determination, and $100 million to spare might have launched a project of this magnitude. But would anyone be able to stop it?

There seems to be a law of nature, if only of human nature, about these things. Either a successful enterprise goes forward or it starts to slide backward; there is no such thing as standing still. As the young men of America came back from the war—Rockefeller's five sons among them—the country launched itself upon the unprecedented program which would shift the economy to a peacetime basis without a sharp recession. In that flush time, the Center's oldest buildings were already of an age that prompted some suspicion that the development was fated to move backward.

15

On the Other Side of the Street

Within the Rockefeller Center family, the complacency of the Last Rivet ceremony had disappeared long before the war's end. Expansion was to be the order of the day, no matter how final the words of 1939 had seemed. By 1945 the direction it would take also had been decided by the needs of a tenant and the acquisition of a piece of land.

The spur to the enterprise was the Standard Oil Company of New Jersey, one of the earliest tenants, which now needed enough room to warrant naming a building for it under its popular appellation of Esso. The real estate that would permit the expansion just happened to be held by still another Rockefeller corporation, Haswin, which had not yet been involved in the Center's construction or operations. It held title as agent for John D. Rockefeller, Jr., to a plot running through from Fifty-first Street to Fifty-second Street, almost directly opposite the north end of Rockefeller Plaza.

With Harrison in Washington as Nelson Rockefeller's chief deputy, the Center's staff architects, Carson & Lundin, drew plans which were completed in time for Haswin to sign a contract for the structural engineering work on March 1, 1945, a little more than two months before the end of the war in Europe. Other negotiations proceeded briskly so that by October 29, the war in the East being ended, too, Standard Oil's lease was signed; the document would make the company the largest of the Center's tenants, topping even the RCA space. The Chemical Bank & Trust Company already had contracted for ground floor quarters.

One feature of the negotiations was a lease on two old houses next door on Fifty-first Street. This was taken in anticipation of the dream that Rockefeller Plaza could be continued through to join the Museum of Modern Art and perhaps a whole new complex of cultural institutions on Fifty-third Street. When they came back after the war, Harrison made some sketches and Nelson Rockefeller made some inquiries, but after three years the project was abandoned as impractical and the leases were surrendered.

Promptly on the cessation of hostilities and the release of men and equipment from war work, the old brownstones on the new site were demolished. Excavation for a thirty-three-story, set-back structure was begun in February, 1946, still under the aegis of Haswin. Just before actual construction started, Rockefeller Center, Inc., formally purchased the land, the contracts and the leases, and officially crossed the street to occupy territory outside the boundaries of Columbia's Upper Estate.

By the time of the opening ceremonies in the fall of 1947 the chairman of the Center's board of directors could report a gratifying profit. (He had resigned the presidency in October, 1945, to be succeeded by Barton P. Turnbull, a member of his father's staff who had been an active member of the board since 1934, serving as treasurer and a vice-president.) In spite of the vastly increased construction costs, the new Esso Building would operate in the black, too.

Obviously, the development was not going to try to stand still. The next step was an attempt to retrieve the losses of the one blighted hope of the original set of buildings, the Center Theater. The lease to NBC for television had never been regarded by the Center's management as more than a temporary expedient which could never return the income needed to support a property of such value. Although its facilities, decor, and seating capacity were still good enough to rank it as one of the premier playhouses in New York, no one was tempted to revive it for either live shows or films.

The decision to tear it down was made by a new managerial team. Turnbull, president for three years, died in 1948 and Executive Manager Robertson retired. Nelson Rockefeller assumed the presidency again; Eyssell was brought over from the Radio City Music Hall to be executive manager and then executive vice-president, and Borella was appointed manager of operations. In 1951, Eyssell succeeded Nelson as president, and two years later when Nelson was appointed under secretary of the new Department of Health, Education, and Welfare by President Eisenhower, his brother Laurance was elected chairman of the board. He was the next younger of the five Rockefellers and had been a member of the Center's board since 1936. More active in its affairs than any of the other three, he had been especially concerned with building plans and had been on most of the important Center committees. He has been chairman ever since, except for a brief term between Nelson's service in the Eisenhower administration and his election as governor of New York.

Laurance's chief business interest had been in aviation, his chief civic interest was conservation. His wartime service had been in the aircraft production branch of the Navy, and he had been one of the organizers of several pioneer companies in the field before and after the war. As chairman of the Center's board, he brought in much of his older brother's administrative talent but in a quieter vein.

His chief colleague and the real executive head of the development was Eyssell. His managerial talent had been proved at the Music Hall; the industry credited him with much of its success, and in the course of his theater career he had acquired a keen understanding of real estate. Theater properties are a very special branch of this business, and it is said that anyone who can deal in them can handle anything. Eyssell was so persuasive that early in his term as executive manager of the Center it was said of him: "He could sell Con Edison's steam service in Hades."

Before Nelson departed for his new job, there had been some discussion of Eyssell's proposal to raze the Center Theater—"after all, the ice had melted," he says—when NBC's lease expired and to look for a tenant to take a major share of an office building on the site. He thought the next-door neighbor, United States Rubber, a likely candidate since it had a considerable number of employees housed in two other New York locations for lack of space in the main office. Also, there was a comfortable backlog of applications from desirable but not quite such big companies.

Laurance Rockefeller announced the decision to demolish the theater in the summer of 1953, but it was almost a year before the wreckers arrived. In that time there were few nostalgic expressions of regret at the passing. In spite of its elegance and its occasional hits, it never had won the hearts of New York. The city seemed more interested in the technical construction problems, which helped account for the delay of a year. The principal complication was the steel frame of one part of the theater which rose nine stories at the corner of Forty-ninth Street and the Avenue of the Americas. It supported one side of the existing Rubber Company Building. Then as the old auditorium had widened out, it abutted on both the eastern wall of the Rubber Company and the western wall of the Eastern Air Lines Building.

Each column and girder had to be studied to see whether it could be torn out or not, and those that remained were carefully stripped of their masonry. The steel for a new nineteen-story structure was fitted to them, with the whole wrapping around two sides of the existing building. Fewer rivets than usual were added to the ten million because the frame was fastened by a new technique of bolts with exceptional tensile strength. At a cost of $11 million the building added 340,000 rentable square feet, and four months before it opened in December, 1955, the last square foot was leased.

At the very outset of Laurance Rockefeller's chairmanship, an even more ambitious expansion plan was under consideration. His father's decision a quarter of a century earlier to put first-class offices west of Fifth Avenue had been an extremely daring venture, some real estate experts had said—foolhardy, others thought. An even riskier proposition, their successors now believed, was to go west of the old Sixth Avenue. The change of name to Avenue of the Americas had not altered the dingy aspect of the street; the demolition of the old elevated had simply exposed the shabbiness of most all the buildings; Rockefeller Center's western façade was the only exception for blocks in either direction. The very shabbiness of the neighbors was a challenge to a successful, well-cared-for enterprise.

At that, the block between Fiftieth and Fifty-first streets was an improvement over most of the others. Once it had been the site of as grim an eyesore as the neighborhood ever saw, for until 1922, stretching west for 410 feet from the avenue, had been a cavernous trolley car barn which housed also repair shops and a power plant. After the demise of the trolley company, the barn had been replaced by a four-story office building facing the avenue, named for its owner Edgar Levy, with a parking lot and some one-story "tax payers" behind. It was a parcel of 82,000 square feet, and in 1953 the Center purchased it as a likely site for future expansion.

Throughout the construction of the United States Rubber Company Addition, the property remained undisturbed. A few months later, as if it could not bear to be without a second big theater, Rockefeller Center also bought the old Roxy between Fiftieth and Fifty-first streets on Seventh Avenue. Its eastern wall ran along the western line of the old car barns. When the deal became public knowledge, there was a rash of speculation that this was going to be the nucleus for a great new "TV City" built by Rockefeller Center and NBC.

In fact, neither the Center nor RCA had such an intention —any longer. The rumor was based on a bit of dead and buried company history. Actually, as soon as the Center bought the Levy property, Eyssell had proposed to Nelson Rockefeller that a project for a television complex be considered. Then he had gone into it at some length with Sarnoff and his associates, who were interested. But no one knew what the future of TV held, not even the man who was still regarded as having the most prophetic vision in broadcasting. It could go all live or all film, all news or all entertainment. The deal for the Roxy was made just in case the cards fell so that NBC would want a batch of great big new studios handy to its executive offices. By the time news of the sale was public, Sarnoff had told Nelson Rockefeller and Eyssell that whatever happened he now knew he was not going to want real estate of this midtown value for any studios to supplement the ones he already had in the RCA Building. This decision became final when it was plain that live TV, which might need a New York audience, would yield to film.

So as the TV City rumor spread, Rockefeller Center already had abandoned the plan and decided upon the use to which it would put the Levy land in its leap across the avenue. The Luce publications were bursting out of the seams of the Time & Life Building and for some months had conducted a quiet survey as to the best possible location for new quarters. After considering a number of spots in and out of the city, the survey committee concluded that the most suitable address for this particular group of magazines was Rockefeller Center. This had been *Time Magazine*'s ninth headquarters; up to then it had averaged a move every two years, and its status now warranted an air of permanence.

No existing structure in the Center would suit, however, so the common interest of the Center with an almost empty site and Time & Life with a desire to keep its address brought them together. The first discussions dealt with the possibility that the magazines might occupy a big share of one of the proposed TV City buildings, but this held scant appeal for *Time Magazine*.

The contract that resulted when NBC lost interest was an innovation for both parties. The publishers wanted to own their building, and so a partnership arrangement, Rockefeller Center's first, was worked out during 1956. A corporation called Rock-Time was organized with the Center owning 55 percent of the stock and Time, Inc., 45 percent. The Center's original investment was $12,100,000 and the publishing firm's was $9,900,000. The rest of the $78,000,000 that the new building would cost—more than half the investment in the first fourteen put together—was borrowed. The offices of the new corporation were divided among some of the leading officials of the sponsors. Thus Eyssell became Rock-Time's president while the chairmanship went to Roy E. Larsen, then president of Time, Inc.

Harrison's firm was engaged to design a forty-eight-story

structure. True to the principle of leaving more open ground than other commercial builders thought they could afford—the Center's ideal is 15 percent—this design kept open a whopping 25½ percent. The architects also made a deliberate departure from the style of the earlier buildings, and even more deliberately worked to achieve a harmony with them. Whether an observer thinks they succeeded or not, the leap across the avenue produced a distinctly more modern look.

That look never could have been achieved in the way it was without that open space, which was left as a broad L-shaped plaza 42 feet wide on Fiftieth Street and 83 feet wide on the avenue. This permitted a rectangular slab without a single setback to rise 587 feet from the center of the plot. Its lean, vertical effect is enhanced by narrow supporting columns encased in limestone soaring straight from street to roof. They are unique in office building construction for they are placed outside the floor area instead of within. The principle is the same as that of the buttresses of a medieval cathedral or, to give a more modern if homely comparison, the outside studs on a railroad boxcar. The practical purpose for the people who are going to use the interior is that their rooms can be perfect rectangles without jogs or jutting angles. The columns also house the duct risers for the air-conditioning system. This system is an unusual one, for it has a special hookup which permits only the magazine cooling to be turned on independently because *Time* and *Life* staffs work Saturday and Sunday.

Harrison's insistence upon flexibility for the space inside is reflected in the exterior walls, which are curtains of glass, metal, and limestone. The intervals between the stone columns are a series of grids of aluminum and clear glass.

The L-shaped plaza is balanced by an L-shaped, seven-story structure which wraps around the base of the tower on the west and north sides and has a landscaped roof terrace. Land-

The new Time & Life Building in a rendering by Hugh Ferriss. The view is from the southeast; the trees are along 50th Street, and the drawing shows traffic flowing along the Avenue of the Americas from right to left. The sketch has added interest as the last such work by one of America's most distinguished architectural artists.

scaping of the plaza and a series of pools there brought the Rockefeller Center penchant for gardens to what was hailed as no longer the wrong side of the Avenue of the Americas.

Before this could be seen in anything but sketches, the revival of the Sidewalk Superintendents Club was a good omen for the popularity of the idea. In May, 1957, the first ground was broken by Nelson Rockefeller and Henry R. Luce, founder of *Time*, operating a pair of pneumatic drills while wearing spotless white work gloves and incongruous business suits. A few weeks later the hole they began was big enough to be worth watching, and the facilities for the watchers included a pavilion with pennants and flowers, model cranes, and plexiglass windows ten feet square. During the next three months, blessed by mostly pleasant weather, a quarter of a million sidewalk superintendents from fifty-one countries signed the register. A great many of them saw relics of the past coming to the surface, because nearly every day at one point the big shovels turned up rails and wheels and pieces of machinery from the streetcar days.

Meanwhile, the architects, not content with mere models, had a two-and-a-half-story mock-up of the façade built on Long Island and later another one to incorporate some changes. After this, Time, Inc., used a six-foot model of the new skyscraper to work out the partitioning and equipping of its fifteen floors—it leased six more for future expansion, but sublet them for the moment. They prepared to use 40 percent of the space, and actually do by now, paying about four times as much rent as they did before they moved.

The whole thing added many statistics to the impressive Rockefeller collection: another 215,000 tons of rock and dirt excavated, although the building set in the resulting hole is estimated to be 15,000 tons lighter; another 32 high-speed elevators carrying 55,000 passengers a day; two off-street truck lifts to pick up the biggest trucks or trailers and carry them to the loading docks in a subbasement where the first truck turn-around ever installed in a building is located; also, 7,000 more windows to wash and 4,700 more locks for which keys can be lost.

By the time the keys were ready for the locks at the end of 1959, the move across the avenue no longer seemed silly to real estate men. Where Rockefeller Center led, the Equitable Life Assurance Society followed, and its new headquarters in the block just north of the Time & Life Building was nearing completion too, just as big but not especially distinguished. A few years more and the Radio City part of Rockefeller Center would really be living up to its name as both the Columbia Broadcasting System and the American Broadcasting Company built on the east side of the avenue above the Center.

If they ever glanced at their furthest west possession, the Center's management might have reflected that places named Roxy did not seem to bring them luck. They were not superstitious, however, and the fact that the theater was hardly a gold mine as a movie palace did not necessarily affect the soundness of their investment. The purpose for which they had bought it was a thing of the past, but they had acquired air and tower rights for the Time & Life Building, which when transferred to Rock-Time, Inc., were priced at $2 million. So the Center could afford to be relaxed about the Roxy's fate in the entertainment world.

Various attempts to revive its old popularity by a couple of lessees, one of whom was Roxy's nephew, were short-lived. They even attempted a combination of stage and screen show, but apparently the Radio City Music Hall has a monopoly on success in this field. Shortly before the Time & Life Building opened, Rockefeller Center had to take over the controls; it was already dickering for an entirely different sort of deal. That deal was consummated in February, 1960, when it was announced that the theater had been sold to Webb & Knapp for an office building, which eventually became the American Management Building. In March the Roxy closed forever.

Tenants were just beginning to move into the Time & Life Building when Rockefeller Center took its next stride. The last one had been carefully thought out and long drawn out too. This one had all the elements of a sudden leap—and in the dark at that—into a big, deep hole.

The hole, two acres of it, belonged to William Zeckendorf, at least it belonged to him as long as he could keep up with lease and tax payments on it. He was a meteoric figure in New York real estate, but his course had passed its zenith and was on the way down. His hole was located on the east side of the Avenue of the Americas, taking up the whole frontage from Fifty-First to Fifty-Second streets facing the new Equitable Building and 450 feet from east to west. It had been dug when Zeckendorf had been planning to build a big new luxury hotel; it would have been the first of any size to be started in New York since before the Depression.

Work had proceeded as far as the excavation and then stopped dead. The huge pit remained, boarded up and eating up costs. Zeckendorf already had approached Eyssell to see if the Center would care to go in with him on completing the project.

"We looked at it very carefully," Eyssell says. "Rockefeller Center always had an idea it would be helpful to the area to have a hotel."

Before negotiations went very far, however, Zeckendorf sold his lease, and the hole, to the Uris Brothers, heads of one of the biggest construction companies in the city. They never had ventured west of Fifth Avenue before, and they had big plans.

Rockefeller Center by now was eager to have a hand in what went up so close to them, and Eyssell, with J. Richardson Dilworth, a Rockefeller financial adviser, entered into talks with Percy Uris. Having just bought a lease, the builders were not keen to sell it, and they did not even want to put up a hotel on this site. They had another plot two blocks up on the other side of the avenue which they preferred for this purpose, and the talks eventually brought Rockefeller Center its second partner.

This one, announced on August 16, 1960, was to be on equal terms, each partner owning 50 percent. For joint risk and profit, they agreed to develop an office building from the Zeckendorf hole and put up the hotel on the other site, which was part of the former William Waldorf Astor estate. An estimated outlay of $150 million was involved, mostly to be borrowed from insurance companies.

The office building had priority because the excavation was there and, anyway, that was of primary interest to both partners. Of course Uris was the builder and Rockefeller Center became the manager. As such, and thanks to its list of applications for space it did not have in its existing buildings, the Center rented most of the 1.7 million square feet by opening day in November, 1962. A year and a half earlier, even before the steel went up, the key lease was negotiated with the Sperry Rand Corporation, which already had a floor in the RCA Building. Its name went on the new building after it took over nearly one quarter of the total.

The design is a forty-three-story slab tower rising from a base with less open space around it than Time & Life, but otherwise somewhat similar. The net effect is to suggest something of a compromise between the Center's old and new styles. Here, as soon as the place opened, a cluster of blue-chip tenants waited to move in.

Meanwhile, the hotel project got underway too. Long before Sperry Rand signed its lease, negotiations for a proper boniface had been started. The Hilton Hotels Corporation was chosen; it was noted for managing high-priced accommodations all over the world. But Laurance Rockefeller thought the operator of this one should be more than that;

on this job, he explained, Rockefeller Center ought to have not one partner but two. He wanted the company responsible for running the hostelry to have capital invested in it.

Laurance was his family's acknowledged expert in this field. Through his conservation and other interests, he already was interested in and involved with hotels in Puerto Rico, the Virgin Islands, and Jackson Hole, Wyoming. Percy Uris was reluctant to be a minority partner; he insisted on retaining 50 percent. So Rockefeller Center relinquished half of its half to Hilton and found itself in the highly novel position of junior partner. One senses a note of pleased surprise in Eyssell's tone when he remarks that it all turned out very well.

"Now there's a place to sleep," he adds, referring to the Center's frequent boast throughout its first thirty years that a man could get just about anything at all there except a bed for the night. "And it brings a lot of people here, too."

In fact, the boast still could be made if one wanted to split a hair. Because the management preserves full membership for property over which it has control, the Hilton Hotel on the Avenue of the Americas is billed as being *at* Rockefeller Center, not *in* it.

It is also rather more hotel than was originally contemplated. Preliminary plans called for a 38-story structure on 80,000 square feet of land. By the time the excavators got to work, the specifications were for 45 stories on 92,000 square feet—it would be another two acres for the Center's statistics except for that difference between *at* and *in*. Its tower, seen from east or west, appears to be of knife-blade thinness. It is 60 feet thick, but does not look it, being 392 feet long and almost 600 feet high.

The dimensions were fixed not so much by aesthetic considerations or a desire to startle but to give each of the 2,200 bedrooms an outside exposure. In the old days this was desirable so the occupants might get some air. But today, in air-conditioned New York, no good hotel wants to expose a sleeper to the city's atmosphere. Most windows are not made for opening but for looking; they may provide light, but their highest function is to give a view of the city.

The appearance of the two buildings owe at least part of their harmony with the Center to the fact that Harrison's firm was a consultant on both. The principal designers, however, were new to the Center—Emery Roth & Sons for the Sperry Rand and William B. Tabler, who had many hotels all over the world to his credit, for the Hilton.

While all this new building was going on to the west and north, Rockefeller Center was also recovering a bit of the old botanical garden which Columbia had sold to the Dutch Reformed Church a century earlier. The lots on Forty-ninth Street which Rockefeller sold to the Massachusetts Mutual Life Insurance Company had been included in a plot on which the company had built an L-shaped, twenty-eight-story building named for its chief tenant, the Sinclair Oil Company. The address, 600 Fifth Avenue, is taken from the one-hundred-foot frontage there running north from Forty-eighth Street. From the avenue the plot runs west for two hundred feet along Forty-eighth Street, and the L is completed by a sixty-three-foot band from the west end of the larger strip right through the block to Forty-ninth Street.

Completed in 1952, this building had been designed by Carson & Lundin to harmonize with Rockefeller Center. In 1960 it became officially part of the Center at a price of $9 million. It worked out at $30 for each rentable square foot of space.

16

The Space Jugglers

If you investigate the operations of Rockefeller Center in search of the secret of its commercial success after the early predictions of doom, you will find that the answer, appearing elusive at the outset, is actually so simple that you did not notice it. For, in fact, there is no secret. The reasons are as plain as the height of the RCA Building or the flowers in the Channel Gardens.

"Rockefeller Center has grown because the tenants have grown," is the way Eyssell puts it, but he also explains why companies do not grow out of the place to some newer building on Madison Avenue or Park Avenue:

As they've expanded, they've asked what we could do for them, and we'd make a feasibility survey of the space. We'd say, 'We can put you here or put you there,' but ultimately they have to have integrated space, perhaps even a building or a part of one.

They want to stay here because we maintain the standards of our tenant relationships. Others think we are extravagant, but we think it is just good business. We like to have our tenants come to us with their problems when they need more space.

Some Rockefeller Center officials like to quote one of their favorite tenants, P. C. Spencer, when he was president of the Sinclair Oil Company. He thought the Center "has developed the art of being a good landlord to such a high state of perfection that a tenant considers himself a guest."

One tenant who could consider itself even more than that and whose presence would keep management officials on their toes if they were inclined to relax is the family of the founder. The fifty-sixth floor of the RCA Building is listed as being occupied by the "Messrs. Rockefeller." Until the death of Mr. Junior on May 11, 1960, this was headquarters for himself as well as for his five sons, whether or not they had offices elsewhere—Nelson in Albany, David at the Chase Manhattan Bank, and so on. Rockefeller himself had moved in from 26 Broadway as soon as the RCA Building was ready. He brought along his comfortable, old-fashioned furniture, too, and his quarters were an incongruous contrast to the varied modern tastes of his children.

The affairs of the Messrs. Rockefeller are so multifarious that their staffs flow out onto other floors, and Rockefeller philanthropic enterprises occupy still additional space. The Rockefeller Foundation was one of the tenants needing expansion that was accommodated in the Time & Life Building.

With all this activity, the owners of Rockefeller Center— their father had turned over title to his sons in 1950—can hardly help being aware of any serious lapses in the standards supposed to make tenants feel like guests. For nearly thirty years either Nelson or Laurance has been president or chairman, and now the next generation is beginning to be active.

The jealousy with which the Center preserves its reputation has led it to protest inferences that other properties are in any way connected with it. In 1962, one of the new neighbors described itself in a circular as being "at Rockefeller Center." A letter to the builders pointed out that this might lead readers to think that the building was in or under the control of the center to the same extent as the Hilton or the Sperry Rand. The phrase was deleted from the propaganda. One indication that the Center has a reputation worth defending in this way is that neighbors do use such phrases as "adjacent to Rockefeller Center" or "in the area of Rockefeller Center."

Reputations of enterprises as big as this are customarily defended by more than lawyers. This is also the function of public relations departments, and Rockefeller Center has one that spends a lot of time, talent, and money to tell the Center's story. Since 1942 it has been headed by Caroline Hood, now a vice-president of Rockefeller Center, Inc., who perhaps has a more personal feeling for her place of employment than she might if she did not happen to be Ray Hood's niece. Among corporate public relations departments, it has its own reputation; newspapermen say it is more concerned than most with news they can use, or as one of them put it: "This is one information department where you can get some information."

Now that the Hilton provides a place to sleep, Rockefeller Center likes to believe it can make room for just about anything you can think of. It has not tried, however, for two items on either end of man's span of life: There is no place to be born, and no place to be buried. No delivery room or maternity ward and no morgue. Not even a chapel or clergyman. But almost anything else, yes.

For example, New York gets its weather predictions from Rockefeller Center. Traditionally, the United States

A 1965 aerial view of the neighborhood of the old Botanic Garden. The Rockefeller Center buildings appear against a background darkened so they are more easily distinguishable. St. Patrick's Cathedral is in the immediate foreground.

Weather Bureau had maintained its local station at the lower tip of Manhattan, for many years on top of the Whitehall Building in Battery Place. But big new skyscrapers downtown interfered with the latest equipment, and finally in the spring of 1959 the bureau decided to install an electronic radar device which, with a clear field, could have a range of 250 miles. A downtown or midtown location was essential, and after conducting a citywide survey, the weather men concluded that Rockefeller Center, specifically the top of the RCA Building, was the most suitable spot.

They were too cautious to sign a lease immediately, however, and Rockefeller Center had some reservations, too. Both wanted an actual trial before committing themselves. The bureau needed to make some tests to be sure the location was as good in practice as it seemed in theory. The Center desired the tests in order to see whether radar operations would interfere with NBC's broadcasts. Also, there was an aesthetic question: Would the weather forecasting apparatus, which had to be protected by a domed housing, mar the appearance of the building?

So before a lease was signed, an experimental operation was agreed upon, and it agitated observant citizens more than a little. On top of the RCA roof a platform eleven feet high was constructed, holding a silvery ball of synthetic fiber eighteen feet in diameter, simulating the dome which in a permanent installation would contain the radar antennas. The public, at least that part of it which looked upward, leaped to the conclusion that this was a brand new contraption for exploring outer space. Hundreds of telephone calls kept the Center's switchboard busy for days.

As a result of the tests, the Weather Bureau learned that it could anticipate some interference from two buildings higher than the RCA, the Empire State and the Chrysler, but not enough to worry about. Rockefeller Center decided that the dome was rather attractive, an interesting addition to the skyline. NBC could not tell that radar was being used. So the Weather Bureau moved in bag and baggage, with the roof installation and with offices way downstairs on the mezzanine. New Yorkers have been getting their weather forecasts from the Center ever since.

In the process of fitting the right tenant into the right space, the staff makes use of a great variety of special skills and knowledge. Its own members have helped install big data processing machines—there are five of them in the Center now. They have put a new main roof on the Music Hall and enlarged and redesigned the United States Passport Bureau's mezzanine space in the International Building because booming business there led to pedestrian traffic problems. They have put new, improved lighting in some buildings, rebuilt and modernized the lobby of the American Metal Climax Building, and hung new bronze doors. Even so, the bill for repairs and maintenance by outside firms is formidable.

Fortunately for the landlord, rents rise with prices. When Time, Inc., moved to its new building and the older one was renamed for the General Dynamics Corporation, a program of reconstruction and rejuvenation was undertaken to fit the needs of the new tenants. As a sign of the changing times after twenty-five years, Eyssell notes that the remodeling cost as much as the original construction.

At that, he thinks he and the tenants got their money's worth. Central air conditioning, new high-speed automatic elevators, flush fluorescent lighting, and closed circuit television facilities were some of the items. A redesigned lobby with elaborate paneling and acoustic hung ceilings were others. The results bear out Wallace Harrison's contention that a well-planned building can be kept up-to-date indefinitely.

At this time and again when the Sperry Rand Building

went up, the innumerable details involved in juggling tenants and space were worked out much as one would solve a complicated jig-saw puzzle. There is nothing specially dramatic or romantic about the job of moving one company into enlarged quarters and renovating the old space for someone else, but the efficiency of this operation is the key to the success of an enterprise such as Rockefeller Center. No office can be allowed to remain vacant for repairs or redecoration too long, nor can it be allowed to remain without the latest facilities. At the same time, the management has to keep track of each of the hundreds of firms renting space so as to be aware of developments which may cause it to expand—new products, new markets, and new services.

When the Time & Life Building opened, twenty-six of the Center's other tenants moved in from six other Rockefeller Center locations, and virtually all of them had been earmarked earlier as about to need new space. Some of the offices they vacated permitted remaining tenants to expand without moving or made way for desirable new companies. The complexities of this operation explain in part why Rockefeller Center, Inc., itself needs a whole floor in The Associated Press Building.

An example of the manifold operations that seem simple, requiring only time and money, but are actually complex is keeping elevators up to date. In 1932, the Center had the fastest high-rise passenger cars in the world, and they held that record for thirty years. But speed and capacity are not the only marks of an elevator system's efficiency. The coordination of the use of cars, so that they serve the floors where heavy traffic develops, is equally important. Delays in opening or closing doors have to be avoided without knocking the passengers about.

Automatic elevators that can do this job satisfactorily are extremely complicated pieces of machinery. Before they can be put together, the managers of a building have to do a lot of studying and figuring. Working out the agreement with the union so no operator would be dismissed was one of the relatively simple problems at the Center; given reasonable good will and mutual confidence it took care of the human element.

There remained the big question of how many cars in any one bank can be taken out of service to be automated. The Center found the answer was one out of four at most. Even more complicated was the study of where traffic is heaviest and when. If you know this, you can set the elevators so they will serve those floors more frequently, not run all the way to the top and come down empty while people are waiting at the halfway level. It is no wonder that elevator automation, initiated in the early 1950's, is not complete in 1965.

This entire project was merely one result of a comprehensive study of manpower, equipment, materials and processes which was conducted under Victor Borella's supervision over a period of three years, ending in 1951. The results were seen in more improvements and efficiencies over the next decade than can very well be so much as listed in a narrative like this.

It may be said that there are three fragile balls of the real estate juggling act which must not be allowed to drop. They are space, tenants, and modernization. The dexterity with which Rockefeller Center has manipulated them has won the admiration of professionals. *Real Estate Forum,* a trade paper, once referred to "Rockefeller Center's passionate predilection for remaining young." In this age of youth, the predilection is hardly notable; what makes the Center unusual is that it does it. The management points out with some pride that more than two hundred office buildings have gone up in New York City since the Center's original fourteen were finished. But no other building in the city, new or old, has as good a record for getting and keeping the blue-chip tenant, they say.

In the long run, any enterprise has to be judged on its record. For a good many years now, the judgment of those who have become well enough acquainted with Rockefeller Center to appraise it intelligently has been favorable. One is tempted to summarize it in terms of its greatest controversy, the painting and destruction of Diego Rivera's mural. What he had planned was perhaps a more exciting, vigorous, and eye-catching work than the one seen there today—most modern artists and connoisseurs would say "undoubtedly" instead of "perhaps." But such a painting inspires either passionate admiration or equally extreme denunciation. It must always be a subject for controversy as long as it commands attention at all.

José Maria Sert's replacement, on the other hand, has attracted neither ardent devotion nor extreme vituperation. His principal mural, which faces you as you walk into the RCA Building's main entrance on Rockefeller Plaza, is meant to depict the development of the United States during three hundred years, not unlike the Rivera concept, but with the conservative viewpoint. Sert has portrayed that process as heroic, dignified, and wholesome; he has symbolized it with conventional figures, men of action and the Muses. Nothing in it remotely resembles the hags who in Rivera's revolutionary painting represented degeneration, gambling, and venereal disease. Artists and philosophers, moralists, and historians could dispute forever as to whether the evil or the good predominated in molding our society. Rockefeller Center seems to me to be a standing argument on one side.

As this book was nearing completion, I took a few minutes to stand in the RCA lobby and look at the mural. I realized that for all the dozens and perhaps hundreds of times I had walked through, this was the first occasion I really was seeing it. It took me by surprise. It did not catch me by the throat as a few masterpieces have done, but it was so eminently satisfying! It is not a painting that will make its creator immortal, I suppose. But it does express a certain restrained power, and the sweep of history—telling us only of the best, perhaps, and therefore not telling the whole story, but leaving us with a reminder of who we are and where we came from.

I went outside and walked around, seeing all of Rockefeller Center in a new light. I thought of the beauty of Manhattan when it was only trees and rocks and Indians. I tried to picture Dr. Hosack's garden and the tourists and students who came here so long ago, the growth of the city as it encompassed and swallowed the idyllic retreat. I remembered it as it had been when I was a New York newspaperman in the 1920's. I paused at the Lower Plaza to smile at Prometheus, who looked very permanent now. I wondered if anywhere else on the island there is a piece of real estate with a story to match this one.

And finally I realized just why I had wanted to write this book. It was because Rockfeller Center is an example of what makes New York a city I have loved—big and bold and busy. It is a place where obviously, in the words of the founder, a maximum income has been developed, but as beautiful as possible, too. Yes, I told myself, that is Little Old New York.

BUILDINGS OWNED AND MANAGED BY ROCKEFELLER CENTER, INC.

Name	Address	Height	Opened
American Metal Climax (originally RKO, then Americas Building)	1270 Avenue of the Americas	409 feet 31 stories	October, 1932
Radio City Music Hall	1260 Avenue of the Americas	121 feet 10 stories	December, 1932
RCA	30 Rockefeller Plaza 49 West 49th Street 50 West 50th Street	850 feet 70 stories	May, 1933
RCA West	1250 Avenue of the Americas	243 feet 16 stories	May, 1933
British Empire	620 Fifth Avenue 10 West 50th Street	90 feet 6 stories	May, 1933
La Maison Francaise	610 Fifth Avenue 9 West 49th Street	90 feet 6 stories	September, 1933
Palazzo d'Italia	626 Fifth Avenue 9 West 50th Street	92 feet 6 stories	May, 1935

ROCKEFELLER CENTER BUILDINGS (continued)

Name	Address	Height	Opened
International North	636 Fifth Avenue 10 West 51st Street	92 feet 6 stories	May, 1935
International	630 Fifth Avenue 45 Rockefeller Plaza 19 West 50th Street 20 West 51st Street	512 feet 41 stories	May, 1935
General Dynamics (originally, Time & Life)	1 Rockefeller Plaza 9 Rockefeller Plaza 15 West 48th Street 14 West 49th Street	490 feet 36 stories	April, 1937
The Associated Press	50 Rockefeller Plaza 34 West 51st Street	226 feet 15 stories	November, 1938
Eastern Air Lines	10 Rockefeller Plaza 35 West 48th Street	225 feet 16 stories	October, 1939
United States Rubber Company	1230 Avenue of the Americas	278 feet 20 stories	April, 1940

ROCKEFELLER CENTER BUILDINGS (continued)

Name	Address	Height	Opened
Esso	15 West 51st Street 22 West 52nd Street	424 feet 33 stories	September, 1947
United States Rubber Company Addition (on site of Center Theater)	61 West 48th Street 60 West 49th Street 1230 Avenue of the Americas	230 feet 19 stories	December, 1955
Time & Life	1271 Avenue of the Americas 111 West 50th Street 121 West 50th Street 110 West 51st Street	587 feet 48 stories	December, 1959
Sperry Rand	1290 Avenue of the Americas 51 West 51st Street 52 West 52nd Street	565 feet 43 stories	November, 1962
Sinclair Oil (purchased by Rockefeller Center, 1963)	600 Fifth Avenue	428 feet 28 stories	January, 1952

SOME FACTS AND STATISTICS
ABOUT THE BUILDINGS OWNED AND MANAGED
BY ROCKEFELLER CENTER, INC.

Land covered, including open space	746,000 square feet or over 17 acres
Assessed real estate valuation	$245,600,000
Real estate taxes paid annually	$ 11,100,000
Rentable space	9,600,000 square feet or 220 acres
Average daily population	208,500
Steam used annually	1,140,805,000 pounds
Water used annually	459,772,000 gallons
Electrical energy used annually	182,222,480 kilowatt hours
Office windows	31,069
Telephones	57,000
Locks	84,750
Elevators	305
Escalators	31

Index

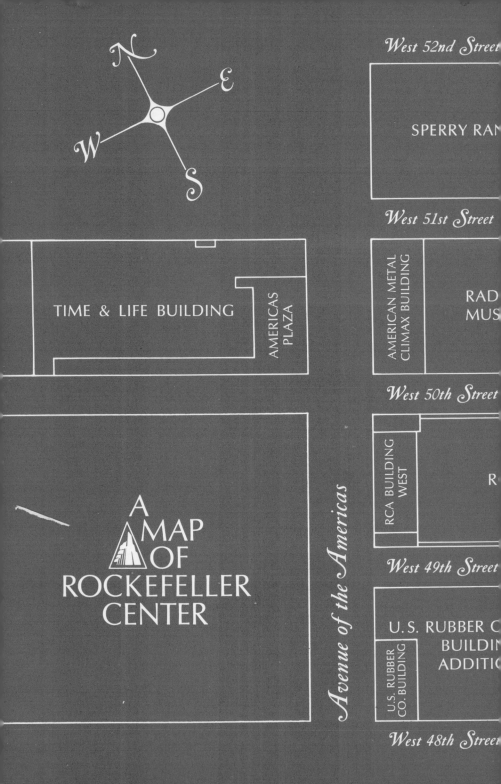

N E W S

West 52nd Street

SPERRY RAN

West 51st Street

AMERICAN METAL CLIMAX BUILDING

RAD
MUS

West 50th Street

RCA BUILDING WEST

R

West 49th Street

U.S. RUBBER C
BUILDIN
ADDITIO

U.S. RUBBER CO. BUILDING

West 48th Street

TIME & LIFE BUILDING

AMERICAS PLAZA

Avenue of the Americas

A MAP OF ROCKEFELLER CENTER